Better Homes and Gardens®

QUILT-LOVERS' FAVORITES®

FROM AMERICAN PATCHWORK & QUILTING®

Better Homes and Gardens® Creative Collection®
Des Moines, Iowa

VOLUME 8

Editorial Director	JOHN RIHA
Editor in Chief	DEBORAH GORE OHRN
Art Director	BRENDA DRAKE LESCH
Managing Editor	KATHLEEN ARMENTROUT

Better Homes and Gardens

QUILT-LOVERS' FAVORITES

FROM AMERICAN PATCHWORK & QUILTING

Group Editor	JENNIFER ERBE KELTNER
Design Director	NANCY WILES
Editors	JILL ABELOE MEAD AND ELIZABETH TISINGER
Senior Graphic Designers	HANNA PIEPEL AND ELIZABETH STUMBO
Staff Writer	JODY SANDERS
Editorial Assistant	MARY IRISH
Contributing Quilt Tester	LAURA BOEHNKE
Contributing Technical Editor	LILA SCOTT
Contributing Editor	JAN RAGALLER
Contributing Graphic Designer and Stylist	JANN WILLIAMS
Contributing Copy Editors	DIANE DORO AND MARY HELEN SCHILTZ
Contributing Proofreader	ANGELA INGLE
Contributing Writer	LISA SCHUMACHER
Contributing Technical Illustrators	CHRIS NEUBAUER GRAPHICS AND KELLY HOLLANDS
Contributing Watercolor Illustrator	ANN WEISS
Color Quality Manager	DALE TUNENDER
Color Quality Analyst	PAM POWERS
Prepress Desktop Specialist	PATRICIA SAVAGE
Photo Studio Manager	JEFF ANDERSON
Consumer Products Marketing Director	STEVE SWANSON
Consumer Products Marketing Manager	WENDY MERICAL
Business Manager	JAMES LEONARD
Production Director	DOUGLAS M. JOHNSTON
Book Production Managers	PAM KVITNE AND MARJORIE J. SCHENKELBERG

Meredith Publishing Group

President	JACK GRIFFIN
Executive Vice President	DOUG OLSON
Editorial Director	MIKE LAFAVORE
Finance and Administration	MIKE RIGGS
Manufacturing	BRUCE HESTON
Consumer Marketing	DAVE BALL
Corporate Sales	JACK BAMBERGER
Interactive Media	LAUREN WIENER
Corporate Marketing	NANCY WEBER
Research	BRITTA WARE

Meredith CORPORATION

President and Chief Executive Officer	STEPHEN M. LACY
Chairman of the Board	WILLIAM T. KERR

In Memoriam – E.T. MEREDITH III, 1933–2003

TREASURED QUILTS

Possibilities. Quilt shops filled with fabric bolts and patterns brim with possibilities for your next quilting project. And if your passion for quilting is as strong as mine, sometimes you needn't look any farther than your own sewing room and fabric stash to create a stunning quilt. No matter where your project begins, there often is a favorite pattern you enjoy making again and again.

That's the premise behind this book series. For our latest edition, Quilt-Lovers' Favorites® Volume 8, we revisit 15 of our readers' favorite patterns from past issues of American Patchwork & Quilting® magazine and sister publications. Then we add to the mix with 29 all-new projects using the blocks, units, borders, or appliqué shapes from the original quilts. You'll find projects large and small—from bed-size quilts to cozy throws, trendy tote bags to table toppers.

As always, full-size patterns, numerous color options, and our reference guide to quiltmaking, Quilter's Schoolhouse, are included to aid you in making these projects. Optional size charts make the math easy, helping you modify the designs to suit your needs.

We hope your passion for quilting is bursting with possibilities as you enjoy this collection of quilts.

Jennifer Keltner

Group Editor, American Patchwork & Quilting

3

TABLE *of* CONTENTS

AGELESS APPEAL
Page **6**

SIGNATURE QUILTS
Page **36**

AGELESS
APPEAL

A classic quilt design, like a classic garment, is

timeless. Its beauty spans generations. Whether it's

the simple elegance of a single block or the complexity

of an art quilt, many of today's quilts have roots in

these ageless designs. Using modern techniques,

re-create the quilts on the following pages to make

quilts future generations will enjoy.

BLOOMING *Lattice*

Challenge your sewing creativity with this historical block that was never named. The block center, a Nine-Patch variation, is surrounded by unusual triangle units.

Materials

3⅞ yards red polka dot (blocks, binding)

3⅛ yards white pin dot (blocks)

2⅞ yards muslin (sashing, border)

5⅓ yards backing fabric

79×96" batting

Finished quilt: 72¼×90"
Finished block: 12" square

Quantities are for 44/45"-wide, 100% cotton fabrics. Measurements include ¼" seam allowances. Sew with right sides together unless otherwise stated.

Cut Fabrics

Cut pieces in the following order. Patterns are on *Pattern Sheet 1*. To make templates of patterns, see Cutting with Templates, *page 153*. Cut border strips lengthwise (parallel to the selvage).

From red polka dot, cut:
- 9—2½×42" binding strips
- 20—5⅛" squares, cutting each diagonally twice in an X for 80 large triangles total
- 40—3⅜" squares, cutting each diagonally twice in an X for 160 small triangles total
- 128—2" squares

- 32—3¼" squares
- 80 of Pattern A
- 80 of Pattern C

From white pin dot, cut:
- 288—2×3¼" rectangles
- 160 of Pattern B

From muslin, cut:
- 2—3¾×90" border strips
- 2—3¾×65¾" border strips
- 31—6¼×12½" sashing strips

Assemble Units

1. Sew red polka dot 2" squares to opposite ends of a white pin dot 2×3¼" rectangle to make a small pieced rectangle **(Diagram 1)**. Press seams toward squares. Repeat to make 64 small pieced rectangles total.

Diagram 1

2. Join white pin dot 2×3¼" rectangles to opposite edges of red polka dot 3¼" square to make a large pieced rectangle. Press seams toward square **(Diagram 2)**. Repeat to make 32 large pieced rectangles total.

Diagram 2

continued

3. Join pieced rectangles to make Unit A (**Diagram 3**). Unit A should be 6¼" square including seam allowances. Repeat to make 32 total of Unit A.

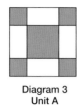

Diagram 3
Unit A

4. Referring to **Diagram 4**, lay out two white pin dot 2×3¼" rectangles, two white pin dot B triangles, one red polka dot A triangle, one red polka dot C piece, and two red polka dot small triangles in sections. Sew together pieces in each section. Press seams toward red polka dot pieces. Join sections to make Unit B. Press seams toward center section. Repeat to make 80 total of Unit B.

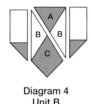

Diagram 4
Unit B

5. Referring to **Diagram 5**, sew red polka dot large triangles to opposite edges of a B unit to make Unit C. Press seams toward red triangles. Repeat to make 40 total of Unit C.

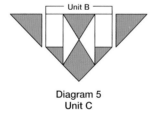

Diagram 5
Unit C

Assemble Blocks

Referring to **Block Assembly Diagram**, sew B units to opposite edges of an A unit. Press seams toward Unit A. Add C units to remaining edges to make a block. Press seams toward Unit A. The block should be 12½" square including seam allowances. Repeat to make 20 blocks total.

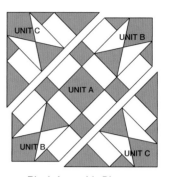

Block Assembly Diagram

Assemble Quilt Top

1. Referring to photo *opposite,* lay out blocks, sashing strips, and remaining A units in nine horizontal rows.

2. Join pieces in each row. Press seams toward sashing strips. Join rows to make quilt center. Press seams toward sashing. The quilt center should be 65¾×83½" including seam allowances.

3. Sew short border strips to short edges of quilt center. Join long border strips to remaining edges to complete quilt top. Press all seams toward border.

Finish Quilt

1. Layer quilt top, batting, and backing; baste. (For details, see Complete the Quilt, *page 159.*)

2. Quilt as desired. The antique quilt shown was hand-quilted with an allover Baptist fan.

3. Using a pencil and a small plate, mark a rounded shape in each corner of the quilt (**Diagram 6**). Trim on marked line. Bind with red polka dot binding strips. (For details, see Complete the Quilt.)

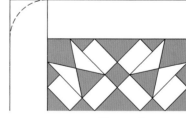

Diagram 6

Blooming Lattice

continued

BLOOMING LATTICE
optional sizes

If you'd like to make this quilt in a size other than for a full-size bed, use the information *below*.

Alternate quilt sizes	Wall/Lap	Twin	King
Number of blocks	9	15	36
Number of blocks wide by long	3×3	3×5	6×6
Additional A units for sashing	4	8	25
Finished size	54½" square	54½×90"	107¾" square

Yardage Requirements			
Red polka dot	2¼ yards	3⅞ yards	6 yards
White pin dot	1½ yards	2½ yards	5¼ yards
Muslin	1⅔ yards	2½ yards	4⅞ yards
Backing	3½ yards	5⅓ yards	9½ yards
Batting	61" square	61×96"	114" square

optional colors

Sizzling Summertime Fun

Quilt tester Laura Boehnke had hot summer days on her mind when she re-created this project using sunny yellows, hot pink, and ocean blue fabrics. The bright, intense colors on a dark background dramatically change the block's look.

FLORAL TABLE TOPPER

Transform a single block into a delightful quilt with a border of cheerful floral fabric.

Materials

⅝ yard green floral (block, outer border, binding)

¼ yard green print (block)

5×15" piece white-and-red print (block)

⅛ yard yellow print (block, inner border)

⅛ yard dark pink print (block)

⅛ yard red print (inner border)

⅞ yard backing fabric

29" square batting

Finished table topper: 22½" square

Cut Fabrics

Cut pieces in the following order. This project uses "Blooming Lattice" patterns on *Pattern Sheet 1*.

From green floral, cut:
- 3—2½×42" binding strips
- 2—4×22½" outer border strips
- 2—4×15½" outer border strips
- 1—3¼" square

From green print, cut:
- 1—5⅛" square, cutting it diagonally twice in an X for 4 large triangles
- 2—3⅜" squares, cutting each diagonally twice in an X for 8 small triangles
- 4—2" squares
- 4 *each* of patterns A and C

From white-and-red print, cut:
- 4—2×3¼" rectangles

From yellow print, cut:
- 8—2×3¼" rectangles
- 4—2" squares

From dark pink print, cut:
- 8 of Pattern B

From red print, cut:
- 4—2×12½" inner border strips

Assemble Block

I. Referring to Assemble Units, *page 9*, steps 1 through 3, make an A unit using green floral 3¼" square, green print 2" squares, and white-and-red print 2×3¼" rectangles.

2. Referring to Assemble Units, Step 4, make four B units using yellow print 2×3¼" rectangles, green print A and C pieces, dark pink print B triangles, and two green print small triangles.

3. Referring to Assemble Units, Step 5, make two C units using B units and green print large triangles.

4. Referring to Assemble Blocks, *page 10*, make one block.

Assemble Quilt Top

I. Sew red print inner border strips to opposite edges of block. Press seams toward border.

2. Add yellow print 2" squares to ends of remaining inner border strips. Press seams toward border strips. Add pieced inner border strips to remaining edges of block. Press seams toward border.

3. Sew short outer border strips to opposite edges of block. Sew long outer border strips to remaining edges to complete quilt top. Press all seams toward outer border.

Finish Quilt

I. Layer quilt top, batting, and backing; baste. (For details, see Complete the Quilt, *page 159.*)

2. Quilt as desired. The featured quilt was machine-stitched with outlining in the triangles, a wavy line through the inner border, and a feathered chain around the outer border.

3. Bind with green floral binding strips. (For details, see Complete the Quilt.)

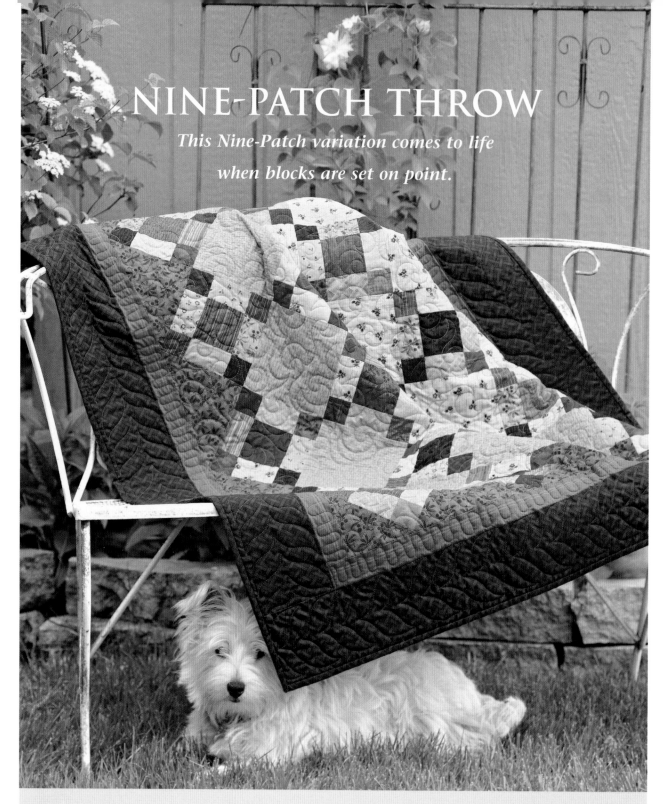

NINE-PATCH THROW

This Nine-Patch variation comes to life

when blocks are set on point.

Blooming Lattice

Materials

I yard total assorted dark prints (blocks)

⅞ yard total assorted light prints (blocks)

½ yard cream print (setting squares)

⅝ yard tan print (setting squares)

⅝ yard brown print (setting and corner triangles)

½ yard red stripe (inner border)

1¾ yards black print (outer border, binding)

3⅞ yards backing fabric

68×76" batting

Finished quilt: 61⅞×69½"

Cut Fabrics

Cut pieces in the following order.

From assorted dark prints, cut:
- 42—3¼" squares
- 168—2" squares

From assorted light prints, cut:
- 168—2×3¼" rectangles

From cream print, cut:
- 12—6¼" setting squares

From tan print, cut:
- 18—6¼" setting squares

From brown print, cut:
- 6—9½" squares, cutting each diagonally twice in an X for 24 setting triangles total (you will use 22)
- 2—5" squares, cutting each in half diagonally for 4 corner triangles total

From red stripe, cut:
- 6—2×42" strips for inner border

From black print, cut:
- 7—5×42" strips for outer border
- 8—2½×42" binding strips

Assemble Quilt Center

1. Referring to Assemble Units, *page 9*, steps 1 through 3, make 42 of Unit A.

2. Referring to photo *right*, lay out A units, cream print setting squares, tan print setting squares, and 22 brown print setting triangles in diagonal rows.

3. Sew together pieces in each row. Press seams toward setting squares. Join rows; press seams in one direction. Add brown print corner triangles to complete quilt center; press seams toward corner triangles. The quilt center should be 49⅜×57½" including seam allowances.

Add Borders

1. Cut and piece red stripe 2×42" strips to make:
- 2—2×57½" inner border strips
- 2—2×52⅜" inner border strips

2. Sew long inner border strips to long edges of quilt center. Join short inner border strips to remaining edges. Press all seams toward inner border.

3. Cut and piece black print 5×42" strips to make:
- 2—5×61⅞" outer border strips
- 2—5×60½" outer border strips

4. Add long outer border strips to long edges of quilt center. Join short outer border strips to remaining edges to complete quilt top. Press all seams toward outer border.

Finish Quilt

1. Layer quilt top, batting, and backing; baste. (For details, see Complete the Quilt, *page 159*.)

2. Quilt as desired. Machine-quilter Kelly Edwards stitched an allover wave pattern across the quilt center and a feather pattern in the outer border.

3. Bind with black print binding strips. (For details, see Complete the Quilt.)

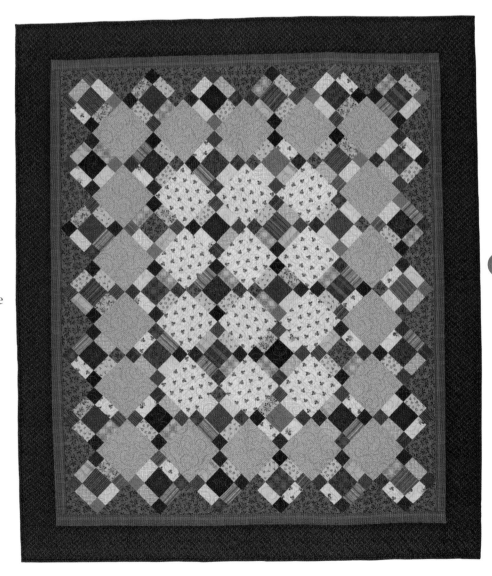

THOUSAND
Pyramids

This century-old quilt is one of many scrap quilts in
shop owner Julie Hendricksen's collection.

Materials

20—18×22" pieces (fat quarters) assorted
    light prints (diamonds, small triangles)

20—18×22" pieces (fat quarters) assorted
    dark prints (diamonds)

4⅝ yards blue plaid (large triangles)

¾ yard solid red (binding)

5 yards backing fabric

88×84" batting

Finished quilt: 81¾×79¼"

Quantities are for 44/45"-wide, 100% cotton fabrics.
Measurements include ¼" seam allowances unless
otherwise noted. Sew with right sides together
unless otherwise stated.

Cut Fabrics

Cut pieces in the following order. Patterns are
on *Pattern Sheet 1*. To make pattern templates,
see Cutting with Templates, *page 153*. Be sure to
transfer dots marked on patterns to templates,
then to fabric pieces. The dots are matching points
and are used to join pieces. *Note:* Patterns A and B
include ½" seam allowances on their short sides.

From *each* assorted light print, cut:
• 6—2×22" strips
From *each* assorted dark print, cut:
• 4—2×22" strips
From blue plaid, cut:
• 120 of Pattern A
• 10 *each* of patterns B and B reversed
From solid red, cut:
• 9—2½×42" binding strips

Assemble Pieced Triangles

Each pieced triangle has a light print and a dark
print. In some cases, the maker of this antique quilt
used the same light print and the same dark print;
in other cases she used more than one light or dark
print. With this in mind, create 20 sets of six light
print and four dark print 2×22" strips each.

    The following instructions use one set of
10 strips to make six pieced triangles. Repeat these
steps to make 120 pieced triangles total.

1. Referring to **Diagram 1** on *page 18*, arrange a set
of ten 2×22" strips into three units, offsetting strips
by approximately 1"; you'll have one light print
strip remaining.

continued

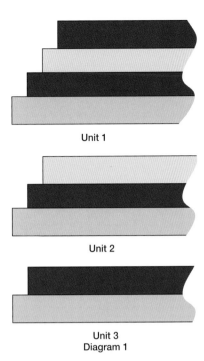

Unit 1

Unit 2

Unit 3
Diagram 1

2. Sew together strips in each unit; press seams toward dark print strips. (Be careful to sew accurate ¼" seam allowances; anything else will result in a distorted or wavy block.) Check width of strips in pieced units. The inside strips should be 1½" wide from seam line to seam line, and outer strips should be 1¾" wide from seam line to raw edge.

3. Trim left-hand edge of each unit at a 45° angle (**Diagram 2**). Cutting parallel to left-hand edge, cut each unit into six 2"-wide sections to make diamond rows. Check every two or three cuts to make sure you are maintaining the 45° angle; correct the angle if needed. Keep diamond rows stacked by unit and label accordingly.

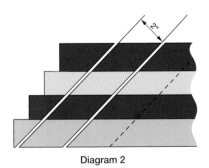

Diagram 2

4. Repeat Step 3 with remaining light print 2×22" strip to cut six single diamond pieces (**Diagram 3**).

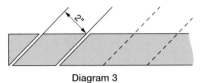

Diagram 3

5. Referring to **Diagram 4** for placement, lay out one diamond row from each unit and one single diamond.

Diagram 4

6. Referring to **Diagram 5**, pin together diamond rows from units 1 and 2, inserting pins into ¼" seam allowances and being careful to intersect seam lines; a small amount of fabric will extend at top and bottom. Slowly sew together rows, removing pins as you reach them. Do not press seams yet.

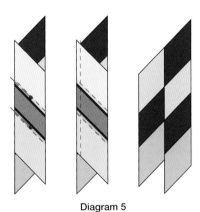

Diagram 5

continued

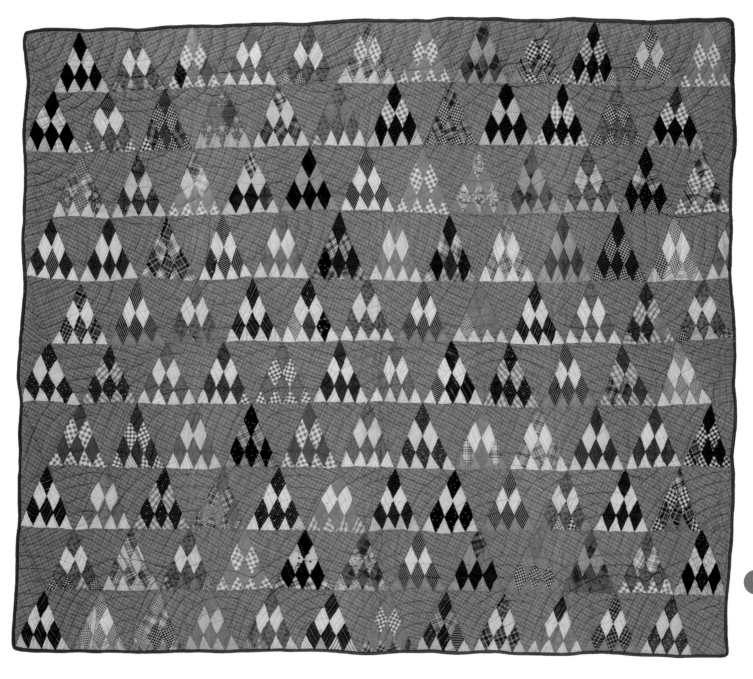

7. Join Unit 3 diamond row and single diamond. Join paired rows. Press seams in one direction; do not press seams open.

8. Referring to **Diagram 6**, place an acrylic ruler over Step 7 pieced unit and trim lower edge ½" below bottom point of each dark diamond to make a pieced triangle. (The additional seam allowance along bottom is needed for piecing quilt top rows together.) Refer to **Diagram 6** to mark matching points along seam line, ¼" from each side edge.

9. Repeat steps 5 through 8 to make six pieced triangles total.

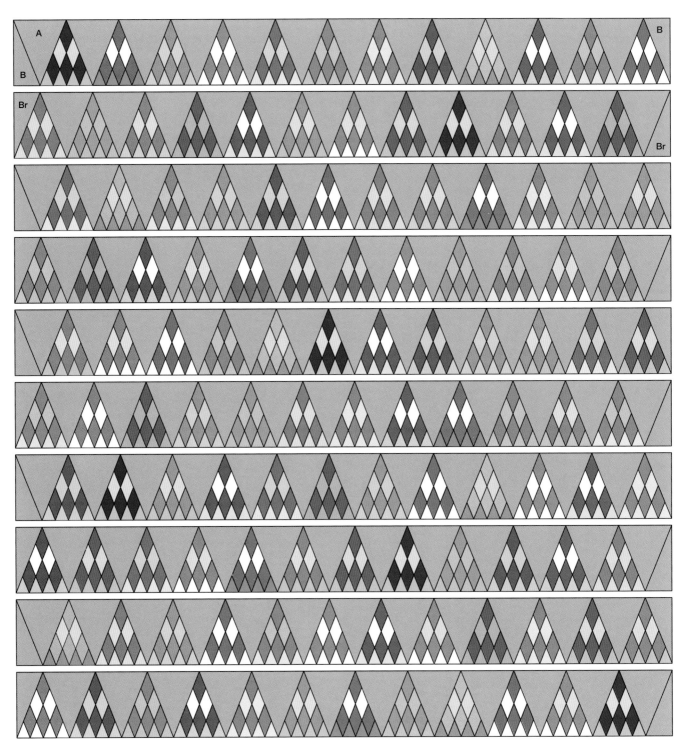

Quilt Assembly Diagram

Thousand Pyramids

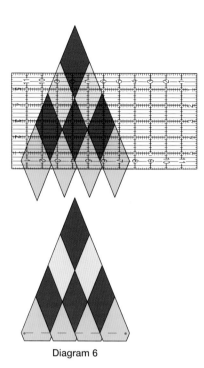

Diagram 6

Assemble Quilt Top

1. Referring to **Quilt Assembly Diagram**, lay out 120 pieced triangles, 120 blue plaid A triangles, 10 blue plaid B triangles, and 10 blue plaid B reversed triangles in 10 horizontal rows.

2. Sew together pieces in each row, carefully aligning matching points. Press seams toward blue plaid triangles. Using ½" seam allowances, join rows to complete quilt top. Press seams toward bottom row.

Finish Quilt

1. Layer quilt top, batting, and backing; baste. (For details, see Complete the Quilt, *page 159.*)

2. Quilt as desired. The antique quilt shown is quilted with a Baptist fan motif of concentric arcs.

3. Bind with solid red binding strips. (For details, see Complete the Quilt.)

optional colors

Subtle Blending

"On the original antique quilt, the pieced triangles had a very deliberate placement of the lights and darks," quilt tester Laura Boehnke says. "I tried to create a scrappier variation using more darks than lights." She kept the background and border on her version monochromatic with a pair of tone-on-tone prints and mixed in an assortment of batiks for the pieced triangles. "I ended up with a few very light fabrics in the pieced triangles," she says. "They almost blend into the background, attracting your eye and making you pause for a moment to see if the pattern is actually repeating, adding interest to the finished quilt."

Thousand Pyramids

PASTEL TABLE RUNNER

Soft colors make this elegant table runner a lovely addition to any room.

Materials

I yard cream print (diamonds, border, binding)

¼ yard *each* cream, gold, green, and blue

  tone-on-tones (diamonds, small triangles)

1⅛ yards backing fabric

19×56" batting

Finished table runner: 12⅜×50"

Cut Fabrics

Cut pieces in the following order.

From cream print, cut:
* 3—2½×42" strips for border
* 4—2½×42" binding strips
* 16—2×22" strips
From cream tone-on-tone, cut:
* 4—2×22" strips
From gold tone-on-tone, cut:
* 8—2×22" strips
From green tone-on-tone, cut:
* 4—2×22" strips
From blue tone-on-tone, cut:
* 8—2×22" strips

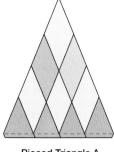

Pieced Triangle A
Diagram 7

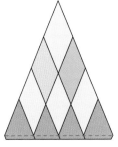

Pieced Triangle B
Diagram 8

Assemble Table Runner Center

1. Referring to Assemble Pieced Triangles, *page 17*, steps 1 through 8, and **Diagram 7**, use cream print, cream tone-on-tone, gold tone-on-tone, and green tone-on-tone 2×22" strips to make eight of Pieced Triangle A, trimming lower edges to leave a ¼" seam allowance.

2. Using blue tone-on-tone strips instead of gold tone-on-tone strips and referring to **Diagram 8**, repeat Step 1 to make seven of Pieced Triangle B.

3. Lay out pieced triangles in a row, starting and ending with Pieced Triangle A (**Quilt Assembly Diagram**). Sew together pieces in row. Press seams in one direction.

4. Trim pieced triangle row to 8⅜×46" including seam allowances to make table runner center.

Add Border

1. Cut and piece cream print 2½×42" strips to make:
* 2—2½×46" border strips
* 2—2½×12⅜" border strips

2. Sew long border strips to long edges of table runner center. Join short border strips to remaining edges to complete table runner top. Press all seams toward border.

Finish Quilt

1. Layer quilt top, batting, and backing; baste. (For details, see Complete the Quilt, *page 159.*)

2. Quilt as desired. The featured quilt is outline-quilted ¼" from the edges of each A and B triangle.

3. Bind with cream print binding strips. (For details, see Complete the Quilt.)

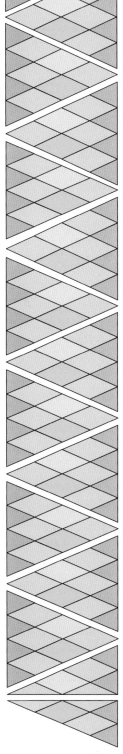

Quilt Assembly Diagram

BOLD BED QUILT

Make a bold statement by using large diamonds in this remarkably colorful quilt.

Materials

12 yards total assorted green, blue, yellow,

and rust prints (blocks)

¾ yard dark green print (binding)

8¼ yards backing fabric

98×101" batting

Finished quilt: 91½×95"

Cut Fabrics

Cut pieces in the following order. This quilt uses "Thousand Pyramids" patterns A and B and two additional patterns, C and D, on *Pattern Sheet 1.*

From assorted green, blue, yellow, and rust prints, cut:
• 149 of Pattern C
• 10 of Pattern D
• 26 of Pattern A
• 2 *each* of patterns B
  and B reversed
From dark green print, cut:
• 10—2½×42" binding strips

Assemble Quilt Top

1. Referring to photo *below*, lay out A, C, and D pieces in 19 diagonal rows.

2. Sew together pieces in each row. Press seams in one direction, alternating direction with each row.

3. Join rows. Press seams in one direction. Add B and B reversed triangles to corners to complete quilt top.

Finish Quilt

1. Layer quilt top, batting, and backing; baste. (For details, see Complete the Quilt, *page 159.)*

2. Quilt as desired. The featured quilt is quilted in an allover feather motif.

3. Bind with dark green print binding strips. (For details, see Complete the Quilt.)

MARINER'S *Compass*

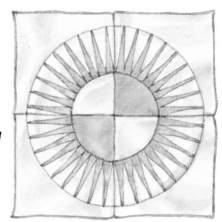

Use foundation piecing to stay on course when assembling this project. Just follow our step-by-step photographs, and you'll consistently stitch the extremely sharp points needed for this traditional pattern.

Materials

8⅔ yards solid yellow (blocks, borders)

14 yards muslin (blocks, borders)

¾ yard multicolor print (binding)

5⅔ yards backing fabric

78×102" batting

Tracing paper

5" square of lightweight cardboard

Finished quilt: 71½×95½"
Finished block: 11" square

Quantities are for 44/45"-wide, 100% cotton fabrics. Measurements include ¼" seam allowances unless otherwise noted. Sew with right sides together unless otherwise stated.

Cut Fabrics

Cut pieces in the following order. Cut border strips lengthwise (parallel to the selvage). Because block units are foundation-pieced, fabric pieces are cut larger than necessary. You'll trim them to the correct size after stitching them to the foundation. Patterns are on *Pattern Sheet 1*. To make templates of

patterns B, C, and D, see Cutting with Templates, *page 153*. Be sure to transfer dots and center points marked on patterns to templates, then to fabric pieces. The dots are matching points and are used to join pieces.

From solid yellow, cut:
• 2—3×88½" inner border strips
• 2—3×66½" inner border strips
• 1,728—1½×4" rectangles
• 4—1½×3" rectangles for outer border
• 96 of Pattern C

From muslin, cut:
• 2—1½×66½" outer border strips
• 1,920—1½×4" rectangles
• 4—3" squares for inner border
• 192 of Pattern B
• 96 of Pattern C

From multicolor print, cut:
• 9—2½×42" binding strips

From lightweight cardboard, cut:
• 1 of Pattern D

Make Foundation Papers

1. Using tracing paper and a pencil, trace Pattern A twenty-four times, tracing all lines and numbers; leave at least 2" between tracings. Place each tracing on top of a stack of eight unmarked sheets of

continued

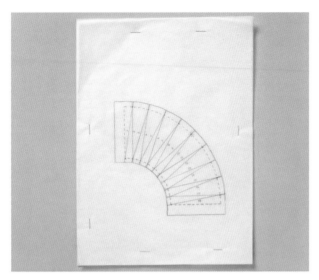

Photo 1

tracing paper. Staple each stack together once or twice on each edge (**Photo 1**).

2. Set up sewing machine with an unthreaded small-gauge needle and 10 to 12 stitches per inch. Sew each stack on traced inner lines through all layers. Do not stitch on traced outer line.

3. Cut out each stack on traced outer line to make 192 perforated foundation papers total.

Assemble Arcs

1. With right sides together, layer a muslin 1½×4" rectangle atop a solid yellow 1½×4" rectangle. Put a perforated foundation paper on top of muslin rectangle, positioning pieces so right edges are a scant ¼" beyond first stitching line and about ⅜" above top of arc (**Photo 2**). Sew on stitching line No. 1. (We used black thread for photographic purposes. When you sew, use a color that matches or blends with your fabrics.)

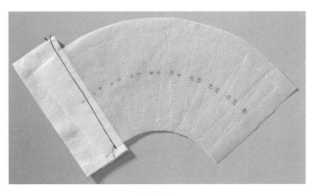

Photo 2

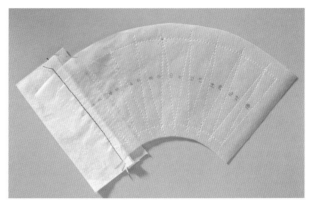

Photo 3

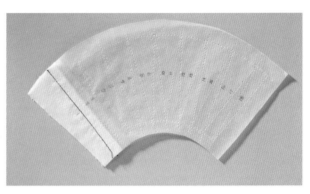

Photo 4

2. Trim seam allowance to a scant ¼". Press rectangles open, pressing seam toward yellow rectangle (**Photo 3**). Trim yellow rectangle to about ¼" beyond stitching line No. 2. Trim pieces even with top and bottom edges of foundation paper (**Photo 4**).

3. Align another muslin 1½×4" rectangle with trimmed yellow piece so their right edges are about ¼" beyond stitching line No. 2. Sew on stitching line No. 2 (**Photo 5**). Trim seam allowance if needed; press seam toward muslin rectangle (**Photo 6**). Trim second muslin rectangle even with top and bottom edges of foundation paper.

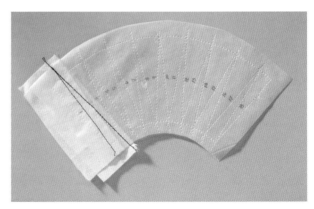

Photo 5

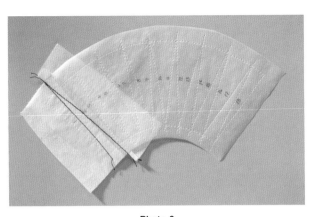

Photo 6

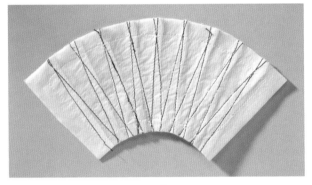

Photo 7

Continue adding rectangles, trimming in same manner, until you've pieced an entire arc (**Photo 7**). With blunt edge of seam ripper, remove foundation paper.

4. Repeat steps 1 through 3 to make 192 pieced arcs total.

Assemble Mariner's Compass Blocks

1. Pin center top of a pieced arc to center bottom of a muslin B piece (centers are marked with Xs on the patterns). Pin at each end. Pin generously in between (**Photo 8**). Sew together by hand or machine, removing each pin just before your needle

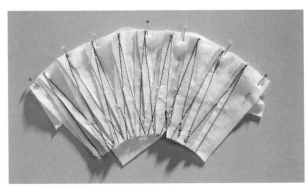

Photo 8

reaches it and sewing a little to the right of the sewing line if necessary to ensure sharp points. Press seams toward muslin B piece. *Note:* If machine-stitching, keep pieced arc on top when you put pieces under the presser foot.

2. Repeat Step 1 with remaining pieced arcs and muslin B pieces.

3. Using ½" seams, sew together four Step 1 units in pairs. Join pairs to make an outer block unit (**Photo 9**). Press all seams open. Repeat to make 48 outer block units total.

4. Using ½" seams, sew together two muslin C pieces and two solid yellow C pieces in pairs. Press seams toward solid yellow pieces. Sew together pairs to make a circle. Press seam in one direction. Trim seam allowances to ¼". Repeat to make 48 circles total.

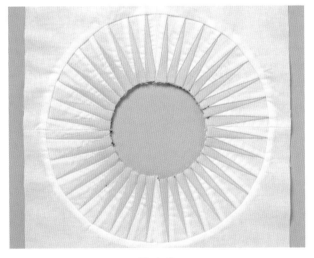

Photo 9

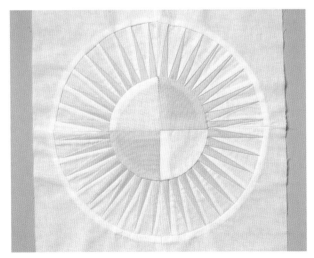

Photo 10

continued

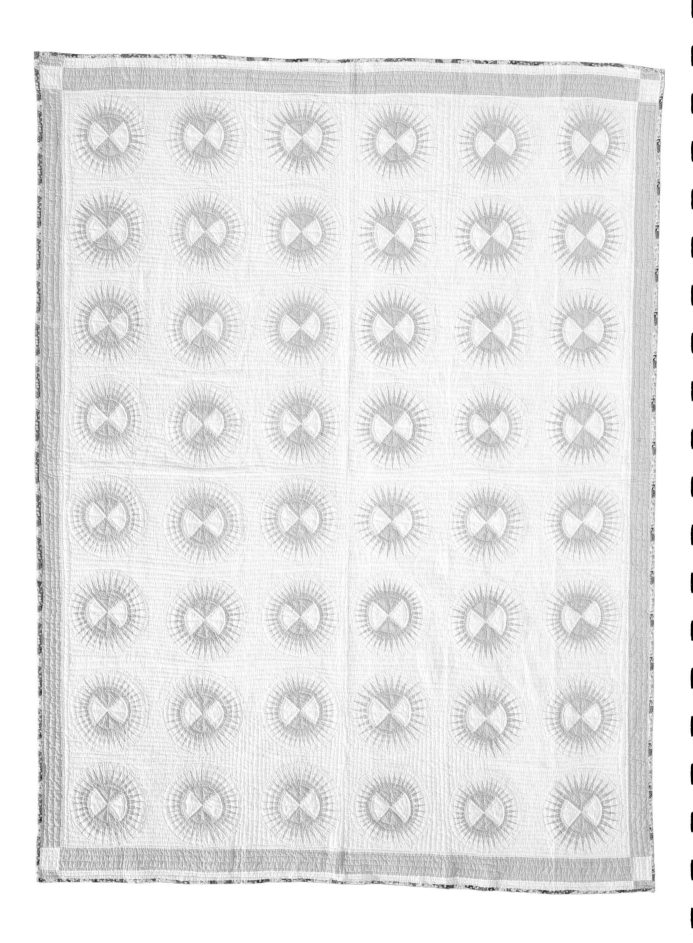

5. Sew a basting stitch a scant ¼" from raw edge of circle. Position cardboard D template on wrong side of circle. Pull up basting stitches, spread gathers out evenly, and gently press to make a block center. Tie thread ends and remove cardboard. Repeat to make 48 block centers total.

6. Appliqué a block center onto each outer block unit to make 48 Mariner's Compass blocks (**Photo 10** on *page 29*). Trim each block to measure 11½" square including seam allowances.

Assemble Quilt Center

Referring to photo *opposite*, lay out blocks in eight horizontal rows. Sew together blocks in each row. Press seams in one direction, alternating direction with each row. Join rows to make quilt center. Press seams in one direction. The quilt center should be 66½×88½" including seam allowances.

Assemble and Add Borders

1. Sew short inner border strips to short edges of quilt center. Press seams toward border.

2. Sew muslin 3" squares to ends of each long inner border strip. Press seams toward border strips. Add pieced long inner border strips to remaining edges of quilt center. Press seams toward border.

3. Sew solid yellow 1½×3" rectangles to ends of each outer border strip. Press seams toward solid yellow rectangles. Sew outer border strips to short edges of quilt center to complete quilt top. Press seams toward outer border.

Finish Quilt

1. Layer quilt top, batting, and backing; baste. (For details, see Complete the Quilt, *page 159.*) Quilt as desired.

2. Bind with multicolor print binding strips. (For details, see Complete the Quilt.)

MARINER'S COMPASS
optional sizes

If you'd like to make this quilt in a size other than for a twin bed, use the information *below*.

Alternate quilt sizes	Wall/Lap	Full/Queen	King
Number of blocks	16	56	81
Number of blocks wide by long	4×4	7×8	9×9
Number of times to trace Pattern A	8	28	41
Place each on stack of eight sheets of tracing paper. There will be four leftover.			
Finished size	49½×51½"	82½×95½"	104½×106½"

Yardage Requirements			
Solid yellow	3¼ yards	10 yards	14 yards
Muslin	5⅜ yards	17¼ yards	24⅜ yards
Multicolor print	½ yard	⅞ yard	⅞ yard
Backing	3⅜ yards	7½ yards	9¼ yards
Batting	56×58"	89×102"	111×113"

optional colors

Bursting at the Seams

When quilt tester Laura Boehnke spotted a black fabric with bursts of color in an allover pattern, she knew it was right for the background in her Mariner's Compass blocks. She selected four coordinating prints, one for each block and for the inner border. Each arc was pieced with a solid navy sateen background.

COMPLEMENTARY PILLOWS

To complete the bedroom decor, we made coordinating pillows—

two small throw pillows and one bed-size pillow.

Materials

2½ yards solid yellow

1½ yards muslin

2—12"-square pillow forms

1 standard-size bed pillow

Tracing paper

5" square of lightweight cardboard

Finished pillows: 13" square, 19×27"

Cut Fabrics

Cut pieces in the following order. This project uses "Mariner's Compass" patterns on *Pattern Sheet 1*.

From solid yellow, cut:
- 2—2×27½" border strips
- 2—19½×16" rectangles
- 2—13½" squares
- 4—1½×11½" border strips
- 156—1½×4" rectangles
- 12 of Pattern B
- 8 of Pattern C
- 4—3" squares
- 4—1½" squares

From muslin, cut:
- 2—3×22½" border strips
- 2—3×11½" border strips
- 4—1½×11½" border strips
- 148—1½×4" rectangles
- 4 of Pattern B
- 8 of Pattern C
- 4—1½" squares

Assemble Mariner's Compass Blocks

Referring to Make Foundation Papers, *page 26*, make 16 foundation papers. Referring to Assemble Arcs on *page 28* and Assemble Mariner's Compass Blocks on *page 29*, make one Mariner's Compass block. Then make three additional Mariner's Compass blocks, reversing the colors.

Assemble Throw Pillows

1. Sew solid yellow 1½×11½" border strips to opposite edges of the Mariner's Compass block with muslin B pieces. Press seams toward border. Join muslin 1½" squares to ends of each remaining solid yellow 1½×11½" border strip. Press seams toward solid yellow strip. Add pieced border strips to remaining edges of block to make a throw pillow top. Press seams toward border.

2. Sew muslin 1½×11½" border strips to opposite edges of Mariner's Compass block with solid yellow B pieces. Press seams toward block. Join solid yellow 1½" squares to ends of each remaining muslin 1½×11½" border strip. Press seams toward solid yellow squares. Add pieced border strips to remaining edges of block to make a second throw pillow top. Press seams toward block.

3. Layer each throw pillow top with a solid yellow 13½"-square pillow back. Sew together, leaving an opening for turning. Turn each right side out; press. Insert a 12"-square pillow form into each opening and whipstitch openings closed.

Assemble Bed-Size Pillow

1. Sew together two remaining Mariner's Compass blocks. Sew muslin 3×22½" border strips to long edges of joined blocks. Sew solid yellow 3" squares to ends of each muslin 3×11½" border strip. Press seams toward solid yellow squares. Join pieced border strips to remaining edges of joined blocks. Press seams toward joined blocks.

2. Sew solid yellow 2×27½" border strips to long edges of joined blocks. Press seams toward solid yellow border.

3. Press under 1" on one long edge of each solid yellow 19½×16" rectangle; stitch. Overlap hemmed edges of rectangles by 4½" to make a 19½×27½" pillow back; baste.

4. Layer pillow top and back. Sew around all edges. Turn right side out; press. Insert standard bed pillow through back opening.

FRAMED SILK BLOCK

Showcase one beautiful block for a classic addition to your decor.

Materials

⅜ yard *each* oriental brocade in red,

    cream, and green (blocks)

⅜ yard lightweight stabilizer (foundation)

5" square of lightweight cardboard

Seam sealant, such as Fray Check (optional)

Cut Fabrics

This project uses "Mariner's Compass" patterns on *Pattern Sheet 1*. Using a seam sealant on the raw edges of fabric that frays easily will keep the project neat and easy to handle during construction.

From red oriental brocade, cut:
- 20—1½×4" strips for blocks
- 2 of Pattern C

From cream oriental brocade, cut:
- 38—1½×4" strips for blocks
- 2 of Pattern B
- 2 of Pattern C

From green oriental brocade, cut:
- 18—1½×4" strips for blocks
- 2 of Pattern B

Assemble Block

1. Referring to Make Foundation Papers (using lightweight stabilizer instead of tracing paper), *page 26,* and Assemble Arcs, *page 28,* use red oriental brocade 1½×4" strips and cream oriental brocade 1½×4" strips to make two pieced arcs total.

2. Repeat Step 1 using cream oriental brocade 1½×4" strips and green oriental brocade 1½×4" strips to make two pieced arcs total.

3. Referring to Assemble Mariner's Compass Blocks, *page 29,* and photo *opposite,* make one Mariner's Compass block.

Frame Block

Mount and insert Mariner's Compass block into frame with 11"-square opening.

Project Tips

To make precisely pieced, intricate blocks, you can sew together fabric scraps on a paper foundation. Some quilters find this technique to be freeing because precise cutting isn't required and grain line direction is not a worry.

When sewing with lightweight, loosely woven fabrics, a seam sealer such as Fray Check will keep raveling to a minimum. For the blocks shown on this page and *opposite,* silk brocade was used. Though silk brocade has a heavier weave than silk, seam sealer still was used on the edges for greater control when handling.

When pressing silk fabric, use a pressing sheet to keep it from stretching or discoloring.

SIGNATURE
QUILTS

Recording political and social occurrences on

quilt blocks was a familiar custom for generations.

Today, documenting a significant event or honoring a

special person with a signature quilt remains popular.

Whether you embroider names with colorful threads

or write them with a permanent marker, use the design

selections in this chapter to create lasting keepsakes

that commemorate the occasions.

REMEMBER
Me

Ohio quiltmaker Lisa DeBee Schiller designed this sweet quilt with her young daughter in mind. Each block contains the name of one of her daughter's favorite toys.

Materials

⅝ yard total assorted purple, green, blue,
  yellow, and tan prints (blocks, border)

¼ yard solid cream (blocks)

⅓ yard pink print (sashing, binding)

26" square backing fabric

26" square batting

Tracing paper

Finished quilt: 20½" square
Finished block: 4" square

Quantities are for 44/45"-wide, 100% cotton fabrics. Measurements include ¼" seam allowances. Sew with right sides together unless otherwise stated.

Piecing Method

Designer Lisa DeBee Schiller foundation-pieced the blocks in this quilt, which means she stitched the pieces together on paper patterns, then removed the papers once the blocks were complete.

For foundation piecing, you need a perforated paper pattern, called a foundation paper, for each block and fabric pieces at least ¼" larger on all sides than the areas they are to cover. The 3" squares and 3×5" rectangles required for this quilt are ample

enough to cover the appropriate places. You don't need to worry about grain lines when cutting out fabric pieces because the foundation papers will provide support.

To foundation-piece, stitch the fabric pieces to a foundation paper with the right side of the foundation paper facing up and fabric pieces underneath. Use a tiny stitch length (12 to 16 stitches per inch) so the paper will easily tear away from the assembled block. Stitch two fabric pieces at a time with right sides together, then press pieces open and trim to size.

Cut Fabrics

Cut pieces in the following order.

From assorted purple, green, blue, yellow, and tan prints, cut:
• 32—3½"-wide rectangles in lengths varying from 2" to 3" for border
• 54—3" squares
From solid cream, cut:
• 9—3×5" rectangles
From pink print, cut:
• 3—2½×42" binding strips
• 2—1×14½" sashing strips
• 4—1×13½" sashing strips
• 6—1×4½" sashing strips

continued

Make Foundation Papers

1. With a pencil, trace Foundation Pattern, found on *Pattern Sheet 2*, on tracing paper once, tracing all lines and numbers. Place the tracing on top of a stack of eight unmarked sheets of tracing paper. Staple stack together once or twice.

2. Set up sewing machine with an unthreaded small-gauge needle and 10 to 12 stitches per inch. Sew paper stack on traced inside lines through all layers. Do not stitch on traced outer line.

3. Cut through stack on traced outer line to make nine perforated foundation papers total.

Foundation-Piece Blocks

1. For one block you'll need one solid cream 3×5" rectangle (signed, if desired); six assorted purple, green, blue, yellow, or tan print 3" squares; and a foundation paper.

2. With wrong sides together, center area No. 1 of a foundation paper over a 3" square **(Diagram 1)**. Remember, this and all subsequent pieces should cover the area within the lines plus ¼" beyond them. Hold fabric piece No. 1 in place with your fingers, a pin, or a dab from a glue stick.

Diagram 1

3. With right sides together, place a second 3" square under first square, aligning raw edges **(Diagram 2)**. With right side of foundation paper up, stitch on line between areas 1 and 2, beginning and ending a few stitches beyond ends of line **(Diagram 3)**. Trim seam allowance to a scant ¼". Press second square open, pressing seam toward area No. 2. Trim pieces to about ¼" beyond lines around areas 1 and 2 **(Diagram 4)**.

Diagram 2   Diagram 3   Diagram 4

4. With raw edges aligned and right sides together, position a solid cream 3×5" rectangle under first two pieces. (Signature on solid cream rectangle should be upside down and facing right side of first two prints.) Stitch on line between areas 1, 2, and 3 **(Diagram 5)**. Trim seam allowance and press solid cream piece open. Trim solid cream piece to about ¼" beyond lines around area No. 3. Add remaining assorted 3" squares in numerical order, trimming and pressing as before, to make a block **(Diagram 6)**.

Diagram 5   Diagram 6

5. Stitch around block edges within ¼" seam allowance area (right outside stitching line). This will help stabilize the block until the quilt top is assembled.

6. Trim block on dashed lines of foundation paper. The block should be 4½" square including seam allowances. Using a seam ripper, carefully tear away foundation paper.

7. Repeat steps 1 through 6 to make nine blocks total.

Assemble Quilt Center

Referring to photo *opposite* for placement, lay out nine blocks, pink print 1×4½" sashing strips, and pink print 1×13½" sashing strips in seven horizontal rows. Sew together pieces in each row. Press seams toward sashing strips. Join rows; press as before. Add pink print 1×14½" sashing strips to sides of pieced rows to complete quilt center. Press seams toward sashing strips.

Assemble and Add Border

1. Cut and piece assorted 3½"-wide rectangles to make:
• 2—3½×20½" border strips
• 2—3½×14½" border strips

2. Sew short border strips to opposite edges of quilt center. Add long border strips to remaining edges to complete quilt top. Press all seams toward border.

Finish Quilt

1. Layer quilt top, batting, and backing; baste. (For details, see Complete the Quilt, *page 159.)*

2. Quilt as desired. Lisa hand-quilted in the ditch around each piece in the blocks and the border.

3. Bind with pink print binding strips. (For details, see Complete the Quilt.)

optional colors

More Ways To Do the Same

Designer Lisa DeBee Schiller enjoys taking a pattern and playing with color placement. Along with the original "Remember Me" quilt shown *opposite* and on *page 38*, Lisa made these two quilts. As you can see, the homespuns *right* and 1930s reproduction prints *below* give each of the finished quilts a different look.

SEEING STARS BED QUILT

The addition of hourglass blocks plus playful color placement

create a warm and inviting bed quilt.

Materials

5¼ yards total assorted cream prints (star blocks)

1¼ yards total assorted pink prints (star blocks)

2 yards total assorted brown prints (star blocks)

1⅝ yards dark pink print (hourglass blocks)

1⅝ yards brown plaid (hourglass blocks)

⅝ yard dark brown print (inner border)

2⅛ yards pink plaid (outer border)

¾ yard pink stripe (binding)

8 yards backing fabric

95" square batting

Tracing paper

Finished quilt: 88½" square
Finished blocks: 8" square

Cut Fabrics

Cut pieces in the following order. This project uses the "Remember Me" pattern on *Pattern Sheet 2*.

From assorted cream prints, cut:
• 820—3" squares
From assorted pink prints, cut:
• 164—3" squares (41 sets of 4)
From assorted brown prints, cut:
• 164—3×5" rectangles (41 sets of 4)
From dark pink print, cut:
• 20—9¼" squares, cutting each diagonally twice in an X for 80 triangles total
From brown plaid, cut:
• 20—9¼" squares, cutting each diagonally twice in an X for 80 triangles total
From dark brown print, cut:
• 8—2½×42" strips for inner border
From pink plaid, cut:
• 10—6½×42" strips for outer border
From pink stripe, cut:
• 9—2½×42" binding strips

Assemble Star Blocks

1. Referring to Make Foundation Papers, *page 40*, make 164 foundation papers total.

2. For one star block you'll need 20 assorted cream print 3" squares, a set of four pink print 3" squares, and a set of four brown print 3×5" rectangles.

3. Referring to Foundation-Piece Blocks, *page 40*, steps 2 through 6, and **Diagram 7** for color placement, make four foundation-pieced blocks total.

Diagram 7

4. Sew together foundation-pieced blocks in pairs (**Diagram 8**). Press seams in opposite directions. Join pairs to make a star block. Press seam in one direction. The block should be 8½" square including seam allowances.

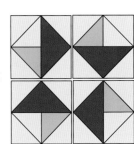

Diagram 8

5. Repeat steps 2 through 4 to make 41 star blocks total.

Assemble Hourglass Blocks

1. Referring to **Diagram 9**, sew together two dark pink print triangles and two brown plaid triangles in pairs. Press seams toward brown plaid triangles.

2. Join pairs to make an hourglass block; press seam in one direction. The block should be 8½" square including seam allowances.

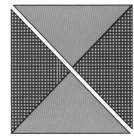

Diagram 9

3. Repeat steps 1 and 2 to make 40 hourglass blocks total.

Assemble Quilt Center

Referring to photo on *page 44*, sew together star blocks and hourglass blocks in nine rows. Press seams toward hourglass blocks. Join rows to make quilt center. Press seams in one direction. The quilt center should be 72½" square including seam allowances.

continued

Add Borders

1. Cut and piece dark brown print 2½×42" strips to make:
- 2—2½×76½" inner border strips
- 2—2½×72½" inner border strips

2. Sew short inner border strips to opposite edges of quilt center. Add long inner border strips to remaining edges. Press all seams toward border.

3. Cut and piece pink plaid 6½×42" strips to make:
- 2—6½×88½" outer border strips
- 2—6½×76½" outer border strips

4. Sew short outer border strips to opposite edges of quilt center. Add long outer border strips to remaining edges to complete quilt top. Press all seams toward outer border.

Finish Quilt

1. Layer quilt top, batting, and backing; baste. (For details, see Complete the Quilt, *page 159.*) Quilt as desired.

2. Bind with pink stripe binding strips. (For details, see Complete the Quilt.)

CHECKERBOARD TOTE BAG

If you have leftover 3" squares from the "Remember Me" quilt,

use them to make this fun tote.

Materials

⅓ yard total assorted cream prints (bag body)

⅓ yard total assorted red and green prints

   (bag body)

⅛ yard green-and-red plaid (bag band)

9×22" piece (fat eighth) red dot (bag band, straps)

⅝ yard cream dot (bag lining)

Finished bag: 10×15×5"

Cut Fabrics

Cut pieces in the following order.

From assorted cream prints, cut:
- 30—3" squares
- 6—2×3" rectangles

From assorted red and green prints, cut:
- 30—3" squares
- 6—2×3" rectangles

From green-and-red plaid, cut:
- 2—3½×15½" strips

From red dot, cut:
- 2—3×22" strips
- 2—1½×15½" strips

From cream dot, cut:
- 2—15½×18½" rectangles

Assemble Bag Body

1. Referring to **Diagram 10**, lay out 15 assorted cream print 3" squares, three assorted cream print 2×3" rectangles, 15 assorted red and green print 3" squares, and three assorted red and green print 2×3" rectangles in six rows, alternating cream with red or green. Sew together pieces in each row. Press seams toward red and green prints. Join rows to make a pieced section. Press seams in one direction. The pieced section should be 14½×15½" including seam allowances. Repeat to make a second pieced section.

2. Join a green-and-red plaid 3½×15½" strip and a red dot 1½×15½" strip along long edges to make a bag band. Press seam toward green-and-red plaid, then topstitch ⅛" from seam line (**Diagram 10**). Repeat to make a second bag band.

3. Referring to **Diagram 10**, sew together a pieced section and a bag band. Press seam toward bag band, then topstitch ⅛" from seam line to make bag front. Repeat to make a matching bag back.

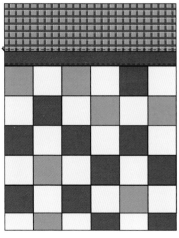

Diagram 10

4. Layer bag front and back; sew together side and bottom edges (**Diagram 11**). Using tip of iron, carefully press seams open.

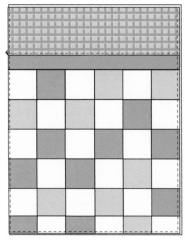

Diagram 11

continued

5. To shape a flat bottom for the bag, at one corner match bottom seam line to side seam line, creating a flattened triangle (**Diagram 12**). Measure and mark on seam allowance 2½" from the point of the triangle. Draw a 5"-long line across triangle, and sew on drawn line. Trim excess fabric. Repeat at remaining bottom corner to make bag body. Turn bag body right side out.

Assemble and Add Straps

Fold a red dot 3×22" strip in half lengthwise and sew together long edges. Turn right side out and press flat; topstitch ⅛" from long edges to make a strap. Repeat to make a second strap.

Referring to **Diagram 13**, pin raw ends of one strap to top edge of bag body front; make sure strap is centered with 4" between the ends. Baste strap ends to bag front a scant ¼" from top edge. Repeat with second strap and bag back.

Assemble Lining

1. Layer two cream dot 15½×18½" rectangles; sew together side and bottom edges, leaving a 6" opening along bottom edge. Using tip of iron, carefully press seam open to make bag lining.

2. Shape a flat bottom for lining as in Assemble Bag Body, Step 5. Leave lining wrong side out.

Assemble Bag

1. Insert bag body inside bag lining with right sides together; straps should be between bag and lining. Align raw edges and seams. Stitch together upper edges of bag body and lining, backstitching over each strap for reinforcement.

2. Turn bag and lining right side out through opening in lining, then pull lining out of bag. Machine-stitch opening of lining closed.

3. Insert lining back into bag and press upper edge. Topstitch ⅛" from upper edge to complete tote bag.

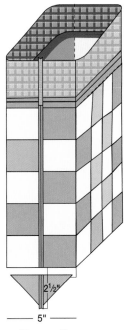

2½"

5"

Diagram 12

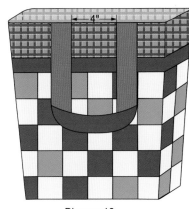

4"

Diagram 13

47

DELECTABLE
Mountains

This scrappy, antique quilt features one print and signature per block.
Make your own version of collector Julie Hendricksen's quilt for a keepsake
that will be cherished for generations.

Materials

3 yards total assorted prints in blue, red, brown,
   gray, tan, and pink (blocks)

3¼ yards muslin (blocks)

5⅝ yards beige dot (setting squares, setting and
   corner triangles, border, binding)

8¼ yards backing fabric

98×105" batting

Finished quilt: 90½×99"
Finished block: 6" square

Quantities are for 44/45"-wide, 100% cotton fabrics.
Measurements include ¼" seam allowances. Sew
with right sides together unless otherwise stated.

Cut Fabrics

Cut pieces in the following order. Setting and
corner triangles are cut larger than necessary. After
assembling quilt center, you'll trim them to fit.

From assorted prints, cut:
- 55—5⅜" squares, cutting each in half diagonally
  for 110 large triangles total

- 330—2⅜" squares, cutting each in half diagonally
  for 660 small triangles total (110 sets of six
  matching small triangles; each set should
  match one large assorted print triangle)

From muslin, cut:
- 55—5⅜" squares, cutting each in half
  diagonally for 110 large triangles total
- 330—2⅜" squares, cutting each in half
  diagonally for 660 small triangles total
- 110—2" squares

From beige dot, cut:
- 10—3×42" strips for border
- 10—2½×42" binding strips
- 10—10½" squares, cutting each diagonally
  twice in an X for 40 setting triangles total
  (you will use 38)
- 90—6½" setting squares
- 2—6" squares, cutting each in half
  diagonally for 4 corner triangles total

Assemble Blocks

1. Sew together a print small triangle
and a muslin small triangle to make a
small triangle-square (**Diagram 1**). Press
seam toward print triangle. The triangle-
square should be 2" square including seam
allowances. Repeat to make six matching
small triangle-squares total.

Diagram 1

continued

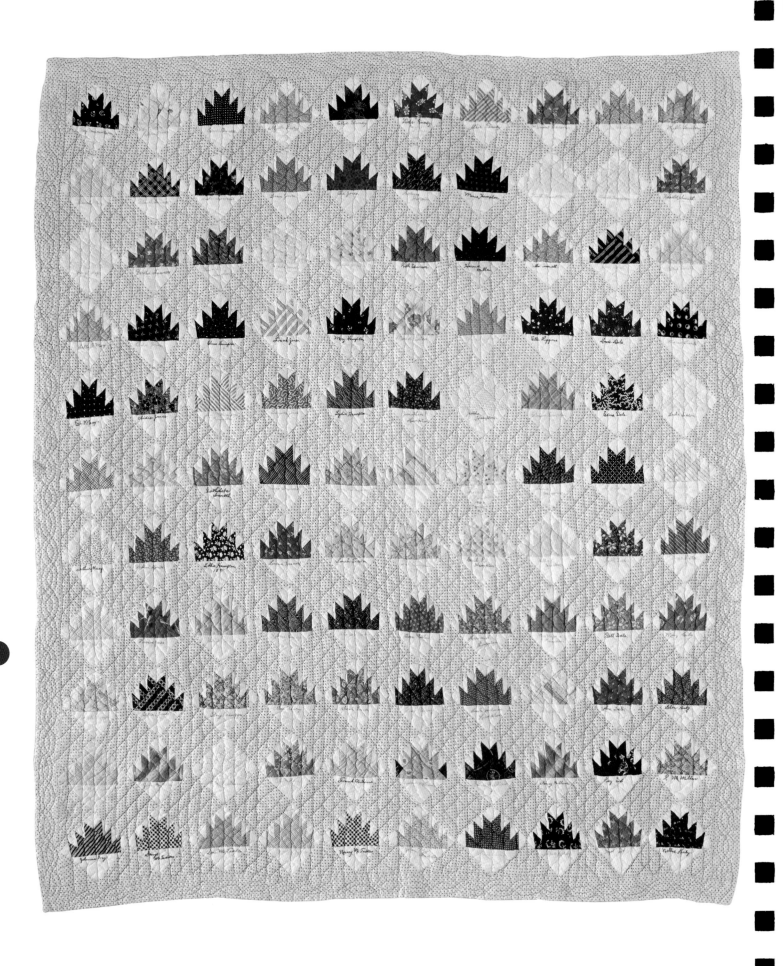

Delectable Mountains

2. Using a large triangle from the same print as used in the small triangle-squares, join a print large triangle and a muslin large triangle to make a large triangle-square. Press seam toward print triangle. The triangle-square should be 5" square including seam allowances.

3. Referring to **Diagram 2**, sew together three small triangle-squares; press seams in one direction. Add joined triangle-squares to a print edge of large triangle-square; press seam toward small triangle-squares.

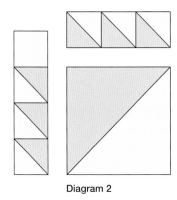

Diagram 2

4. Join a muslin 2" square and three remaining small triangle-squares; press as before. Add to remaining print edge of large triangle-square to make a Delectable Mountains block **(Diagram 2)**. Press seam toward large triangle-square. The block should be 6½" square including seam allowances.

5. Repeat steps 1 through 4 to make 110 Delectable Mountains blocks total.

Assemble Quilt Center

1. Referring to photo *opposite*, lay out 110 Delectable Mountains blocks, 90 beige dot 6½" setting squares, and 38 beige dot setting triangles in diagonal rows.

2. Sew together pieces in each row. Press seams in one direction, alternating direction with each row. Join rows; press seams in one direction. Add beige dot corner triangles to complete quilt center.

3. Trim quilt center to 85½×94", leaving a ¼" seam allowance beyond block corners.

Add Border

1. Cut and piece beige dot 3×42" strips to make:
• 2—3×94" border strips
• 2—3×90½" border strips

2. Sew long border strips to long edges of quilt center. Then add short border strips to remaining edges to complete quilt top. Press seams toward border.

Finish Quilt

1. Layer quilt top, batting, and backing; baste. (For details, see Complete the Quilt, *page 159*.)

2. Quilt as desired. The quiltmaker hand-quilted this project in a 1½"-wide diagonal grid. A cable design is showcased in the border.

3. Bind with beige dot binding strips. (For details, see Complete the Quilt.)

continued

optional colors

Bold and Beautiful

Quilt tester Laura Boehnke used brightly colored batiks to bring this century-old quilt design into the present. She reversed the placement of light and dark fabrics, eliminating the need for signatures and allowing the blocks to blend into the background.

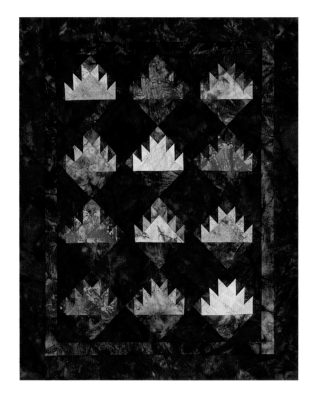

optional sizes

If you'd like to make this quilt in a size other than for a full-size bed, use the information *below*.

Alternate quilt sizes	Crib/Wall	Twin	King
Number of blocks	30	63	144
Number of blocks wide by long	5×6	7×9	12×12
Number of setting squares	20	48	121
Number of setting triangles	18	28	44
Finished size	48×56½"	65×82"	107½" square

Yardage Requirements

	Crib/Wall	Twin	King
Yards total of assorted prints in blue, red, brown, gray, tan, and pink	1¼ yards	2 yards	3⅞ yards
Muslin	1¼ yards	2⅛ yards	4¼ yards
Beige dot	2⅜ yards	4⅛ yards	8½ yards
Backing	3 yards	5 yards	9½ yards
Batting	54×63"	71×88"	114" square

BORDERED CAFÉ CURTAIN

Adorn a simple purchased café curtain for a colorful accent in the kitchen.

Materials

¼ yard *each* red and green prints

Two purchased café curtain panels

Cut Fabrics

Cut pieces in the following order. The instructions are for 28"-wide café curtain panels. If your curtain measurements are different, adjust the number of triangle-squares and length of folded border strips as needed to fit the curtains.

From *each* red and green print, cut:
• 2—2½×29" strips
• 19—2⅜" squares, cutting each in half diagonally for 38 triangles total

Assemble and Add Borders

1. Referring to Assemble Blocks, *page 49*, Step 1, use red and green print triangles to make 38 triangle-squares total. Press seams toward red print.

2. Lay out 19 triangle-squares in a row (**Diagram 3**). Sew together pieces to make a triangle-square row. Press seams in one direction. Repeat to make a second triangle-square row.

Diagram 3

3. With wrong side inside, fold a red print 2½×29" strip in half lengthwise; press. Aligning raw edges, sew folded red print strip to green edge of triangle-square row. Press seam open. Repeat to add a green print 2½×29" strip to remaining long edge of triangle-square row (**Diagram 4**).

Diagram 4

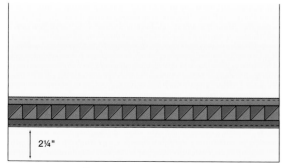

2¼"

Border Placement Diagram

4. Place bordered triangle-square row on café curtain panel 2¼" from bottom hem (**Border Placement Diagram**). Turn short ends of bordered triangle-square row under ¼", then topstitch all edges in place using matching thread. *Note:* If necessary, measure your curtain and adjust the amount turned under at each end of the triangle-square row to match the exact curtain width.

5. Repeat steps 3 and 4 to add border to remaining café curtain panel.

CIVIL WAR THROW

Arrange blocks into a Forest Path pattern for a whole new look. Civil War-era reproduction fabrics enhance the antique feel of this terrific throw-size quilt.

Materials

1¾ yards black paisley (blocks, border, binding)

9—18×22" pieces (fat quarters) assorted blue, green, red, and black prints (blocks)

2⅝ yards tan print (blocks)

1¼ yards brown print (sashing)

¼ yard red floral (sashing, border)

3⅞ yards backing fabric

69×83" batting

Finished quilt: 63½×77"
Finished block: 12" square

Cut Fabrics

Cut pieces in the following order.

From black paisley, cut:
• 7—4×42" strips for border
• 7—2½×42" binding strips
• 4—5⅜" squares, cutting each in half diagonally for 8 large triangles total
• 24—2⅜" squares, cutting each in half diagonally for 48 small triangles total

From *each* fat quarter, cut:
• 4—5⅜" squares, cutting each in half diagonally for 8 large triangles total
• 24—2⅜" squares, cutting each in half diagonally for 48 small triangles total

From tan print, cut:
• 40—5⅜" squares, cutting each in half diagonally for 80 large triangles total
• 240—2⅜" squares, cutting each in half diagonally for 480 small triangles total
• 80—2" squares

From brown print, cut:
• 49—2×12½" sashing rectangles

From red floral, cut:
• 4—4" squares
• 30—2" sashing squares

Assemble Pinwheel Units

1. Referring to Assemble Blocks, *page 49,* steps 1 and 2, make six matching small triangle-squares and one large triangle-square.

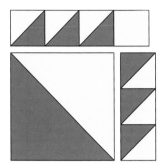

2. Referring to Assemble Blocks, Step 3, and **Diagram 5**, make a Delectable Mountains block; notice how print half of large triangle-square points away from small triangle-squares.

Diagram 5

3. Repeat steps 1 and 2 to make four matching Delectable Mountains blocks total. Sew together blocks in pairs (**Diagram 6**). Press seams in opposite directions. Join pairs to make a pinwheel unit. Press seam in one direction. The pinwheel unit should be 12½" square including seam allowances.

Diagram 6

4. Repeat steps 1 through 3 to make 20 pinwheel units total.

Assemble Quilt Center

1. Referring to photo *above right,* lay out 20 pinwheel units, 49 brown print sashing rectangles, and 30 red floral sashing squares in 11 rows.

2. Sew together pieces in each row. Press seams toward sashing rectangles. Join rows to make

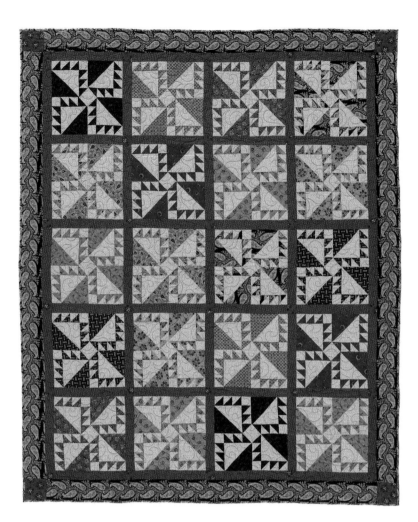

quilt center. Press seams toward sashing rows. The quilt center should be 56×69½" including seam allowances.

Assemble and Add Border

1. Cut and piece black paisley 4×42" strips to make:
• 2—4×69½" border strips
• 2—4×56" border strips

2. Sew short border strips to short edges of quilt center. Press seams toward border.

3. Sew red floral 4" squares to opposite ends of long border strips. Press seams toward border strips. Add long borders to remaining edges of quilt center to complete quilt top. Press seams toward border.

Finish Quilt

1. Layer quilt top, batting, and backing; baste. (For details, see Complete the Quilt, *page 159.*)

2. Quilt as desired. A wave pattern was machine-quilted across the featured quilt top.

3. Bind with black paisley binding strips. (For details, see Complete the Quilt.)

CROWDED *Lake*

While on vacation, designer Kris Kerrigan had friends sign strips of fabric backed by freezer paper. Later, she worked the signature strips into simple patchwork blocks. The finished quilt brings to mind a throng of canoes filling a waterfront, rekindling for Kris fond memories of warm days.

Materials

⅓ yard light blue print (blocks)

16—⅛-yard pieces assorted dark plaids and stripes in gold, red, blue, brown, green, and purple (blocks, outer border)

16—⅛-yard pieces assorted plaids, solids, and stripes in cream and tan (blocks, outer border)

¼ yard brown stripe (inner border)

¼ yard brown check (binding)

37" square backing fabric

37" square batting

Fine-point permanent marking pen: black

Freezer paper

Perle cotton No. 8: taupe

Finished quilt: 30½" square
Finished block: 6" square

Quantities are for 44/45"-wide, 100% cotton fabrics. Measurements include ¼" seam allowances. Sew with right sides together unless otherwise stated.

Cut Fabrics

Cut pieces in the following order.

From light blue print, cut:
• 16—3⅞" squares, cutting each in half diagonally for 32 triangles total

From *each* assorted dark plaid or stripe, cut:
• 2—1⅞×4¾" rectangles
• 1—3⅞" square, cutting it in half diagonally for 2 triangles total
• 7—1½×2½" rectangles (you will use 104 of the 112 rectangles)

From one dark brown plaid, cut:
• 4—2½" squares

From *each* assorted cream or tan plaid, solid, or stripe, cut:
• 1—2×4¾" rectangle

From remaining assorted cream or tan plaids, solids, and stripes, cut:
• 224—1½" squares

continued

From brown stripe, cut:
• 2—1½×26½" inner border strips
• 2—1½×24½" inner border strips
From brown check, cut:
• 3—2½×42" binding strips
From freezer paper, cut:
• 16—1½×4¼" rectangles

Create Signature Strips

1. Center shiny side of a freezer paper 1½×4¼" rectangle on wrong side of a cream or tan 2×4¾" rectangle; press. Repeat with remaining freezer paper and cream and tan rectangles.

2. Have friends use a black fine-point permanent marking pen to sign fabric side of prepared strips, making sure they don't write in the seam allowances, to make signature strips. Remove freezer paper. (Designer Kris Kerrigan recommends preparing a few extra strips in case someone makes a mistake.)

Assemble Blocks

1. For one block you'll need one signature strip, two light blue print triangles, and one set of two 1⅞×4¾" rectangles and two triangles in the same dark plaid or stripe.

2. Sew dark plaid or stripe 1⅞×4¾" rectangles to opposite edges of signature strip (**Diagram 1**) to make a block center. Press seams toward dark rectangles. The block center should be 4¾" square including seam allowances.

Diagram 1

3. Referring to **Diagram 2**, sew dark plaid or stripe triangles to side edges of block center. Press seams toward triangles.

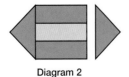

Diagram 2

4. Sew light blue print triangles to top and bottom edges of block center to make a signature block (**Diagram 3**). Press seams toward light blue

triangles. The block should be 6½" square including seam allowances.

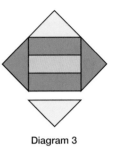

Diagram 3

5. Repeat steps 1 through 4 to make 16 signature blocks total.

Assemble Quilt Center

Referring to photo *opposite* for placement, lay out signature blocks in four rows. Sew together blocks in each row. Press seams in one direction, alternating direction with each row. Join rows to make quilt center. Press seams in one direction. The quilt center should be 24½" square including seam allowances.

Add Inner Border

Sew short brown stripe inner border strips to opposite edges of quilt center. Add long brown stripe inner border strips to remaining edges. Press all seams toward inner border.

Assemble and Add Outer Border

1. Use a pencil to mark a diagonal line on wrong side of each cream or tan plaid, solid, or stripe 1½" square.

2. Align a marked cream or tan square with one corner of a dark plaid or stripe 1½×2½" rectangle (**Diagram 4**; note direction of drawn line). Stitch on drawn line; trim excess fabric, leaving ¼" seam allowance. Press open attached triangle. Sew a second marked cream or tan square to opposite end of the dark rectangle (**Diagram 4**; again note direction of drawn line). Trim and press as before to make a Flying Geese unit. The unit should be 1½×2½" including seam allowances. Repeat to make 104 Flying Geese units total.

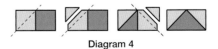

Diagram 4

3. Align a marked cream or tan 1½" square with one corner of a dark brown plaid 2½" square (**Diagram 5;** note direction of drawn line). Sew on drawn line; trim excess fabric, leaving ¼" seam allowance. Press open attached triangle. Sew a marked cream or tan square to each remaining corner of dark brown plaid square, trimming and pressing as before, to complete a corner unit. The unit should be 2½" square including seam allowances. Repeat to make four corner units total.

Diagram 5

4. Referring to photo *below*, join 26 Flying Geese units to make an outer border strip. Press seams open. Repeat to make four outer border strips total.

5. Add outer border strips to opposite edges of quilt center. Press seams toward inner border.

6. Sew corner units to ends of remaining outer border strips. Press seams toward corner units. Add pieced outer border strips to remaining edges to complete quilt top. Press seams toward inner border.

continued

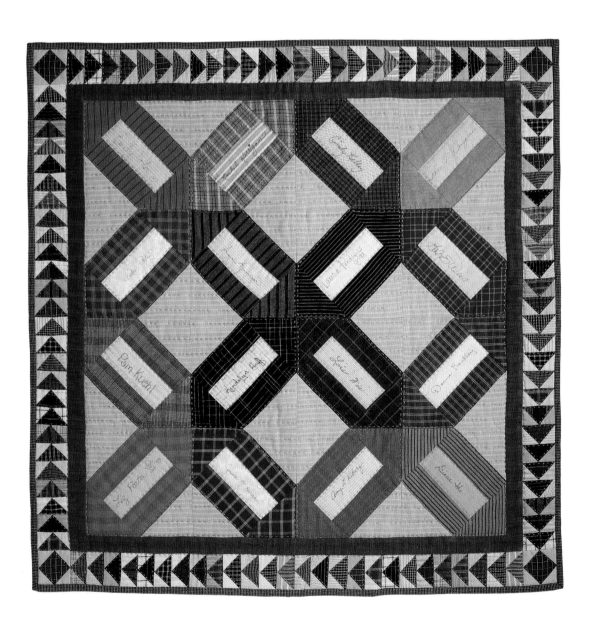

Finish Quilt

1. Layer quilt top, batting, and backing; baste. (For details, see Complete the Quilt, *page 159.)*

2. Quilt as desired. Kris used taupe perle cotton and long, primitive stitches to hand-quilt just inside the edges of each block, signature strip, Flying Geese triangle, and corner unit. Kris also quilted horizontal lines on each light blue print triangle to resemble water ripples.

3. Bind with brown check binding strips. (For details, see Complete the Quilt.)

optional colors

Straight As An Arrow

Instead of seeing canoes in the block as designer Kris Kerrigan did, quilt tester Laura Boehnke saw arrows. By simply placing red or blue fabrics in the center signature strip and in the triangles at either end of the strip, Laura created an arrow.

LONG PILLOW

Flying Geese accents and nautical themed fabric team up for this oversized pillow.

Materials

⅛ yard total assorted blue prints

    (Flying Geese units)

⅛ yard total assorted red and cream prints

    (Flying Geese units)

1½ yards sailboat print (pillow, flange)

14×28" pillow form

Finished pillow: 34×20"

Cut Fabrics

Cut pieces in the following order.

From assorted blue prints, cut:
- 56—1½" squares

From assorted red and cream prints, cut:
- 28—1½×2½" rectangles

From sailboat print, cut:
- 2—19½×20½" rectangles
- 2—3½×38" rectangles
- 2—3½×24" rectangles
- 1—16½×14½" rectangle
- 2—4½×14½" rectangles

Assemble Flying Geese Units

1. Referring to Assemble and Add Outer Border, *page 58*, steps 1 and 2, use assorted blue print 1½" squares and assorted red and cream print 1½×2½" rectangles to make 28 Flying Geese units.

2. Aligning long edges, sew together 14 Flying Geese units to make a Flying Geese row. Press seams open. Repeat to make a second Flying Geese row.

Assemble Pillow Front

1. Referring to **Pillow Front Assembly Diagram**, sew together two Flying Geese rows, two sailboat print 4½×14½" rectangles, and the sailboat print 16½×14½" rectangle to make pillow center. Press seams toward sailboat print.

2. Matching center points and beginning and ending seams ¼" from edge, sew sailboat print 3½×24" rectangles to short edges of pillow center. Repeat to add sailboat print 3½×38" rectangles to remaining edges of pillow center, mitering corners, to make pillow front. (For details, see Mitered Border Corners, *page 156*.)

Finish Pillow

1. Turn under ¼" twice along one long edge of each sailboat print 19½×20½" rectangle; stitch hem in place. Overlap hemmed edges by 3½" and baste to make a 34½×20½" pillow back.

2. Layer pillow front and pillow back. Stitch around all edges. Turn right side out through back opening; press.

3. Stitch in the ditch around pillow center through all layers, backstitching at overlap on pillow back. Insert pillow form through back opening to complete pillow.

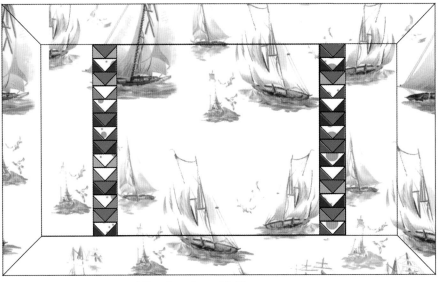

Pillow Front Assembly Diagram

HAPPY BABY QUILT

*Cheery and playful fabrics
make this simple block come to life.
Add a few signatures and you've
created a memory quilt.*

Materials

3¼ yards total assorted pink, green, blue, red,

yellow, and cream prints (blocks)

⅞ yard pink print (border)

½ yard solid pink (binding)

3½ yards backing fabric

61" square batting

Finished quilt: 54½" square

Cut Fabrics

Cut pieces in the following order.

From assorted pink, green, blue, red, yellow, and
cream prints, cut:
• 128—3⅞" squares, cutting each in half
  diagonally for 256 triangles total
• 64—2×4¾" rectangles
• 64 sets of two matching 1⅞×4¾"
  rectangles
From pink print, cut:
• 6—3½×42" strips for border
From solid pink, cut:
• 6—2½×42" binding strips

Assemble Quilt Center

1. Referring to Assemble Blocks,
page 58, steps 1 through 4, use assorted
print 2×4¾" and 1⅞×4¾" rectangles
and triangles to make 64 signature
blocks total.

2. Referring to **Quilt Assembly
Diagram,** lay out 64 blocks in eight
rows. Sew together blocks in each
row. Press seams in one direction,
alternating direction with each row.
Join rows to make quilt center. Press
seams in one direction. The quilt center
should be 48½" square including seam
allowances.

Add Border

1. Cut and piece pink print 3½×42" strips to make:
• 2—3½×54½" border strips
• 2—3½×48½" border strips

2. Sew short border strips to opposite edges of
quilt center. Join long border strips to remaining
edges to complete quilt top. Press all seams toward
border.

Finish Quilt

1. Layer quilt top, batting, and backing; baste.
(For details, see Complete the Quilt, *page 159.*)

2. Quilt as desired. A large leaf design was
machine-stitched across the featured quilt top.

3. Bind with solid pink binding strips. (For details,
see Complete the Quilt.)

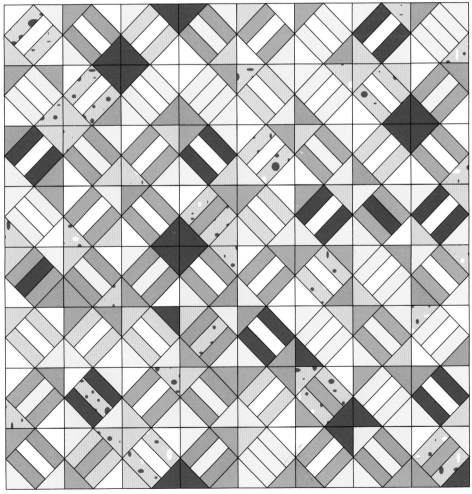

Quilt Assembly Diagram

COLORFUL CREATIONS

The colors in a quilt are often what you notice first,

even before identifying the pattern. Fabric choices

make a dramatic difference in a quilt's appearance.

Push your boundaries and add a personal touch to

the colorful quilts in this chapter by experimenting

with fabric colors and intensities outside your

usual range. Create quilts that grab attention

from the moment you see them.

Pink
Pinwheels

*Piece O' Cake designers Becky Goldsmith and Linda Jenkins
created a delightful quilt that children of all ages can enjoy.*

Materials

2¼ yards total assorted black-and-white prints

    (appliqué foundations, borders)

1⅝ yards total assorted pink prints

    (appliqués, borders)

Scraps of assorted blue prints (appliqué centers)

1⅛ yards pink stripe (borders, binding)

2¾ yards backing fabric

49×59" batting

Finished quilt: 42½×52½"
Finished block: 10" square

Quantities are for 44/45"-wide, 100% cotton fabrics.
Measurements include ¼" seam allowances. Sew
with right sides together unless otherwise stated.

Cut Fabrics

Cut pieces in the following order. Patterns are on
Pattern Sheet 2. To make templates of the patterns,
see Cutting with Templates, *page 153.*

From assorted black-and-white prints, cut:
- 9—12" squares
- 12—6¼" squares
- 4—3" squares
- 45—2½" squares
- 74—1½×2½" rectangles

From assorted pink prints, cut:
- 96 of Pattern A
- 45—2½" squares
- 74—1½×2½" rectangles
- 4 of Pattern B

From assorted blue print scraps, cut:
- 12 of Pattern B

From pink stripe, cut:
- 8—1½×42" strips for borders
- 1—23" square, cutting it into enough 2½"-wide
  bias strips to total 200" in length for binding
  (For details, see Cutting Bias Strips, *page 157.*)

Assemble Appliqué Blocks

1. Sew together four
black-and-white print
6¼" squares in pairs
(Diagram 1). Press seams
in opposite directions.

2. Join pairs to make
a pieced appliqué
foundation. Press seam
in one direction. The
appliqué foundation should be
12" square including seam allowances.

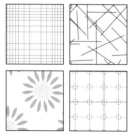

Diagram 1

continued

3. Repeat steps 1 and 2 to make three pieced appliqué foundations total.

4. Referring to **Appliqué Placement Diagram**, arrange eight pink print A pieces and one blue print B piece on each black-and-white print 12"-square appliqué foundation and on each pieced 12"-square appliqué foundation; baste in place.

Appliqué Placement Diagram

5. With matching thread and working from bottom layer to top, hand-appliqué pieces to foundations. Press finished appliqués from the wrong side.

6. Trim each appliquéd foundation to 10½" square, including seam allowances, to make 12 appliquéd blocks total.

7. Center a pink print B piece on each black-and-white print 3" square (**Diagram 2**); baste. With matching thread, appliqué pieces to squares; press. Trim each appliquéd square to 2½" square, including seam allowances, to make four appliquéd border corners total.

Diagram 2

Assemble Quilt Center

1. Referring to **Quilt Assembly Diagram**, lay out 12 appliquéd blocks in four horizontal rows.

2. Sew together pieces in each row. Press seams in one direction, alternating direction with each row. Join rows to make quilt center. Press seams in one direction. The quilt center should be 30½×40½" including seam allowances.

Assemble and Add Borders

1. Cut and piece pink stripe 1½×42" strips to make:
• 2—1½×48½" border No. 3 strips
• 2—1½×42½" border No. 1 strips
• 2—1½×36½" border No. 3 strips
• 2—1½×30½" border No. 1 strips

2. Sew short border No. 1 strips to short edges of quilt center. Add long border No. 1 strips to long edges. Press all seams toward border.

3. Aligning long edges, sew together 16 pink print 1½×2½" rectangles and 16 black-and-white print 1½×2½" rectangles, alternating colors, to make a short border No. 2 strip. Press seams toward pink prints. The short border No. 2 strip should be 2½×32½" including seam allowances. Repeat to make a second short border No. 2 strip.

4. Join two appliquéd border corners, 21 pink print 1½×2½" rectangles, and 21 black-and-white print 1½×2½" rectangles to make a long border No. 2 strip. Press seams toward pink prints. The long border No. 2 strip should be 2½×46½" including seam allowances. Repeat to make a second long border No. 2 strip.

5. Sew short border No. 2 strips to short edges of quilt center. Add long border No. 2 strips to long edges. Press all seams toward border No. 1.

6. Sew short border No. 3 strips to short edges of quilt center. Add long border No. 3 strips to remaining edges. Press all seams toward border No. 3.

7. Sew together 10 pink print 2½" squares and nine black-and-white print 2½" squares to make a short border No. 4 strip. Press seams toward pink prints. The short border No. 4 strip should be 2½×38½" including seam allowances.

8. Repeat Step 7 using nine pink print 2½" squares and 10 black-and-white print 2½" squares to make a second short border No. 4 strip.

9. Referring to **Quilt Assembly Diagram**, sew short border No. 4 strips to short edges of quilt center. Press seams toward border No. 3.

10. Join 13 pink print 2½" squares and 13 black-and-white print 2½" squares to make a long border No. 4 strip. Press seams toward pink prints. The long border No. 4 strip should be 2½×52½" including seam allowances. Repeat to make a second long border No. 4 strip.

11. Referring to **Quilt Assembly Diagram** for placement, sew long border No. 4 strips to long edges of quilt center to complete quilt top. Press seams toward border No. 3.

Finish Quilt

1. Layer quilt top, batting, and backing; baste. (For details, see Complete the Quilt, *page 159.*)

2. Quilt as desired. Each flower appliqué is hand-quilted with a spiral in the center and zigzags in the petals. The borders are quilted with geometric diamonds and squares.

3. Bind with pink stripe bias binding strips. (For details, see Complete the Quilt.)

continued

1½×30½"

1½×42½"

1½×36½"

1½×48½"

Quilt Assembly Diagram

PINK PINWHEELS
optional sizes

If you'd like to make this quilt in a size other than for a wall hanging, use the information *below*.

Alternate quilt sizes	Twin	Full/Queen	King
Number of blocks	35	56	100
Number of blocks wide by long	5×7	7×8	10×10
Finished size	62½×82½"	82½×92½"	112½" square

Yardage Requirements			
Total assorted black-and-white prints	5 yards	7⅓ yards	12⅜ yards
Total assorted pink prints	2⅞ yards	4 yards	6½ yards
Total assorted blue prints	⅛ yard	¼ yard	⅓ yard
Pink stripe	1½ yards	1⅔ yards	2 yards
Backing	5 yards	7½ yards	10 yards
Batting	69×89"	89×99"	119" square

HOMESPUN TABLE TOPPER

Warm homespun plaids give this quick-and-easy centerpiece an old-fashioned appeal.

Materials

⅔ yard total assorted green, blue, purple, rust, tan, and black plaids (border Nos. 2 and 4)

26" square light green plaid (center)

⅓ yard pink plaid (border Nos. 1 and 3)

⅜ yard rust stripe (binding)

1¼ yards backing fabric

42" square batting

Finished table topper: 36" square

Cut Fabrics

Cut pieces in the following order.

From assorted green, blue, purple, rust, tan, and black plaids, cut:
• 72—2½" squares
• 104—1½×2½" rectangles

From light green plaid, cut:
• 1—24½" square

From pink plaid, cut:
• 2—1½×32½" border No. 3 strips
• 2—1½×30½" border No. 3 strips
• 2—1½×26½" border No. 1 strips
• 2—1½×24½" border No. 1 strips

From rust stripe, cut:
• 4—2½×42" binding strips

Assemble Table Topper

1. Referring to **Quilt Assembly Diagram**, join 26 assorted 1½×2½" rectangles to make a short border No. 2 strip. Repeat to make a second short border No. 2 strip.

2. Join 26 assorted 1½×2½" rectangles and two 2½" squares to make a long border No. 2 strip. Repeat to make a second long border No. 2 strip.

3. Sew together 16 assorted 2½" squares to make a short border No. 4 strip. Repeat to make a second short border No. 4 strip.

4. Sew together 18 assorted 2½" squares to make a long border No. 4 strip. Repeat to make a second long border No. 4 strip.

5. Using pink plaid border Nos. 1 and 3 strips and previously stitched border Nos. 2 and 4 strips, join borders, top and bottom first, in numerical sequence to light green plaid 24½" square to complete quilt top. Press seams as directed in Assemble and Add Borders, *page 68.*

Finish Quilt

1. Layer quilt top, batting, and backing; baste. (For details, see Complete the Quilt, *page 159.)*

2. Quilt as desired. An allover feather design is machine-stitched across this table topper.

3. Bind with rust stripe binding strips. (For details, see Complete the Quilt.)

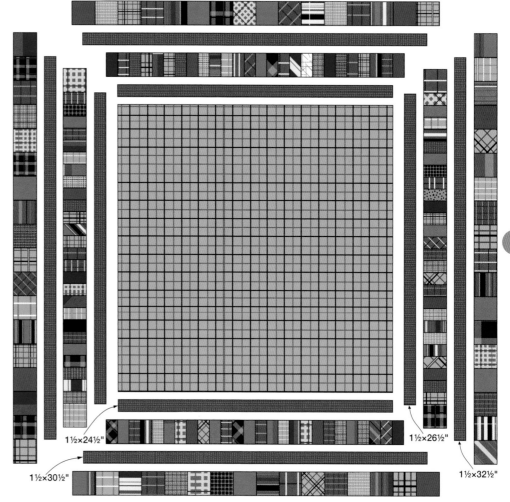

1½×24½"

1½×26½"

1½×30½"

1½×32½"

Quilt Assembly Diagram

FUNKY FLOWERS BED QUILT

Whimsical and bright, this fun and easy quilt is sure to delight.

Materials

- 6¼ yards total assorted pink, blue, green, purple, and yellow prints and stripes (blocks, appliqués)
- ⅓ yard *each* light pink, light blue, and light yellow prints (appliqué foundations)
- 1¼ yards multicolor stripe (border, binding)
- 7¼ yards backing fabric
- 87×101" batting
- 1 yard lightweight fusible web
- Machine-quilting thread: green

Finished quilt: 80½×94½"

Cut Fabrics

Cut pieces in the following order. This project uses "Pink Pinwheels" patterns on *Pattern Sheet 2*. To achieve same petal orientation, Pattern A will need to be reversed for fusible web appliqué. To use fusible web for appliquéing, complete the following steps.

1. Lay fusible web, paper side up, over patterns. Use a pencil to trace each pattern the number of times indicated in cutting instructions, leaving ½" between tracings. Cut out each fusible-web shape roughly ¼" outside traced lines.

2. Following manufacturer's instructions, press fusible-web shapes onto wrong sides of designated fabrics; let cool. Cut out fabric shapes on drawn lines. Peel off paper backings.

From assorted pink, blue, green, purple, and yellow prints and stripes, cut:
• 53—10½" squares
• 44—5½" squares
• 64 of Pattern A (16 sets of 4 matching A petals)
From assorted yellow prints, cut:
• 8 of Pattern B
From *each* light pink, light blue, and light yellow print, cut:
• 3—10½" squares (you will use 8)
From multicolor stripe, cut:
• 4—2½×42" strips for border
• 9—2½×42" binding strips

Assemble Four-Patch Blocks

Referring to Assemble Appliqué Blocks, *page 67*, steps 1 and 2, use assorted pink, blue, green, purple, and yellow print and stripe 5½" squares to make 11 Four-Patch blocks. Each block should be 10½" square including seam allowances.

Appliqué Blocks

1. Referring to **Appliqué Placement Diagram**, lay out four A petals from one print, four A petals from a second print, and one yellow print B flower center on a light pink, light blue, or light yellow print 10½" square. Fuse all pieces in place.

Appliqué Placement Diagram

2. Using green thread and working from bottom layer to top, machine-blanket-stitch around each appliqué piece to complete an appliquéd block. The block should be 10½" square including seam allowances.

3. Repeat steps 1 and 2 to make eight appliquéd blocks total.

Assemble Quilt Top

1. Cut and piece multicolor stripe 2½×42" strips to make:
• 2—2½×80½" border strips

2. Referring to photo *below*, lay out appliquéd blocks, multicolor stripe border strips, Four-Patch blocks, and 53 assorted pink, blue, green, purple, and yellow print and stripe 10½" squares in 11 rows.

3. Sew together pieces in each row. Press seams in one direction, alternating direction with each row. Join rows to complete quilt top. Press seams in one direction.

Finish Quilt

1. Layer quilt top, batting, and backing; baste. (For details, see Complete the Quilt, *page 159.*)

2. Quilt as desired. Machine-quilter Kelly Edwards stitched a spiral design using variegated thread across the quilt top.

3. Bind with multicolor stripe binding strips. (For details, see Complete the Quilt.)

HEADING
North

Designer Mabeth Oxenreider's quilt makes a bold statement with batik Flying Geese blocks set in vertical rows.

Materials

2½ yards total assorted batiks (blocks)

2 yards bright blue print (sashing, border, binding)

3⅛ yards backing fabric

55×67" batting

Finished quilt: 48½×60½"

Quantities are for 44/45"-wide, 100% cotton fabrics. Measurements include ¼" seam allowances. Sew with right sides together unless otherwise stated.

Cut Fabrics

Cut pieces in the following order. Cut sashing and border strips lengthwise (parallel to the selvage).

From assorted batiks, cut:
- 64—3½×6½" rectangles
- 128—3½" squares (64 sets of 2 matching squares)

From bright blue print, cut:
- 4—6½×48½" border strips
- 3—4½×48½" sashing strips
- 6—2½×42" binding strips

Assemble Flying Geese Units

1. Using a pencil, mark a diagonal line on wrong side of each batik 3½" square.

2. Referring to **Flying Geese Diagram**, align a marked batik square with one end of a batik 3½×6½" rectangle; note placement of marked line. Stitch on marked line. Trim excess fabric, leaving a ¼" seam allowance. Press open attached triangle. In same manner, sew a matching marked batik square to opposite end of batik rectangle to make a Flying Geese unit. The unit should be 3½×6½" including seam allowances. Repeat to make 64 Flying Geese units total.

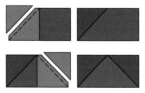

Flying Geese Diagram

Assemble Quilt Center

1. Referring to photo *opposite* for placement, lay out Flying Geese units in four vertical rows. Sew together units in each row. Press seams in one direction. Each Flying Geese row should be 6½×48½" including seam allowances.

continued

2. Sew together three bright blue print 4½×48½" sashing strips and four Flying Geese rows to make quilt center. Press seams toward sashing strips. The quilt center should be 36½×48½" including seam allowances.

Add Border

1. Sew bright blue print border strips to long edges of quilt center. Press seams toward border.

2. Sew remaining bright blue print border strips to remaining edges to complete quilt top. Press seams toward border.

Finish Quilt

1. Layer quilt top, batting, and backing; baste. (For details, see Complete the Quilt, *page 159*.) Quilt as desired.

2. Bind with bright blue print binding strips. (For details, see Complete the Quilt.)

HEADING NORTH
optional sizes

If you'd like to make this quilt in a size other than for a wall hanging, use the information *below*.

Alternate quilt sizes	Twin	Full/Queen	King
Number of Flying Geese units	120	224	320
Number of units wide by long	5×24	8×28	10×32
Number of sashing strips	4	7	9
Finished size	58½×84½"	88½×96½"	108½" square

Yardage Requirements

Total assorted batiks	4¼ yards	7⅔ yards	10⅔ yards
Bright blue print*	3¼ yards	5 yards	6½ yards
Backing fabric	5⅛ yards	8 yards	9⅝ yards
Batting	65×91"	95×103"	115" square

*Unlike the original quilt, blue print yardages are for cutting sashing and border strips the width of the fabric, then piecing them to correct length.

JEWELED CLASSIC BED QUILT

Arrange Flying Geese units to form Broken Dishes blocks, then add sashing

and corner squares to give this quilt a completely new look.

Materials

5 yards total assorted red, orange, blue, purple, green, and brown prints (blocks, border corners)

5 yards total assorted tan prints (blocks)

2½ yards gold print (sashing)

1⅓ yards navy blue print (sashing squares, border corners, binding)

2⅛ yards blue stripe (border)

8¾ yards backing fabric

105" square batting

continued

Finished quilt: 98½" square
Finished block: 12" square

Cut Fabrics
Cut pieces in the following order.

From assorted red, orange, blue, purple, green, and brown prints, cut:
- 144—3½×6½" rectangles
- 72—3⅞" squares, cutting each in half diagonally for 144 triangles total
- 144—3½" squares

From assorted red prints, cut:
- 8—3½×6½" rectangles for border corners

From gold print, cut:
- 84—2½×12½" sashing strips

From navy blue print, cut:
- 10—2½×42" binding strips
- 16—3½" squares for border corners
- 49—2½" sashing squares

From blue stripe, cut:
- 10—6½×42" strips for border

Cut and Assemble Blocks
From one tan print, cut:
- 2—3½×6½" rectangles
- 2—3⅞" squares, cutting each in half diagonally for 4 triangles total
- 8—3½" squares

1. Referring to Assemble Flying Geese Units, *page 75*, and **Diagram 1**, use assorted red, orange, blue, purple, green, and brown print rectangles and the tan print squares to make four dark Flying Geese units (top Flying Geese unit in **Diagram 1**). In same manner, use assorted red, orange, blue, purple, green, and brown print squares and tan print rectangles to make two light Flying Geese units (bottom Flying Geese unit in **Diagram 1**).

Diagram 1   Diagram 2

2. Sew together a red, orange, blue, purple, green, or brown print triangle and a tan print triangle to make a triangle-square (**Diagram 2**). Press seam away from tan print. The triangle-square should be 3½" square including seam allowances. Repeat to make four triangle-squares total.

3. Referring to **Block Assembly Diagram**, lay out four dark Flying Geese units, two light Flying Geese units, and four triangle-squares in rows. Sew together pieces in each row. Press seams in one direction, alternating direction with each row. Join rows to make a block. Press seams in one direction. The block should be 12½" square including seam allowances.

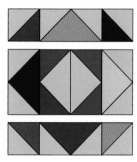

Block Assembly Diagram

4. Repeat cutting instructions and steps 1 through 3 to make 36 blocks total.

Assemble Quilt Top
1. Referring to photo *opposite*, lay out 36 blocks, 84 gold print 2½×12½" sashing strips, and 49 navy blue print 2½" sashing squares in rows.

2. Sew together pieces in each row. Press seams toward sashing strips. Join rows to make quilt center. Press seams toward sashing rows. The quilt center should be 86½" square including seam allowances.

3. Cut and piece blue stripe 6½×42" strips to make:
- 4—6½×86½" border strips

4. Sew border strips to opposite edges of quilt center. Press seams toward border.

5. Using a red print rectangle and two navy blue print 3½" squares, repeat Step 1 in Cut and Assemble Blocks to make a border Flying Geese unit. Repeat to make eight border Flying Geese units total.

6. Join two border Flying Geese units to make a border corner (**Diagram 3**). Press seam in one direction. Repeat to make four border corners total.

Diagram 3

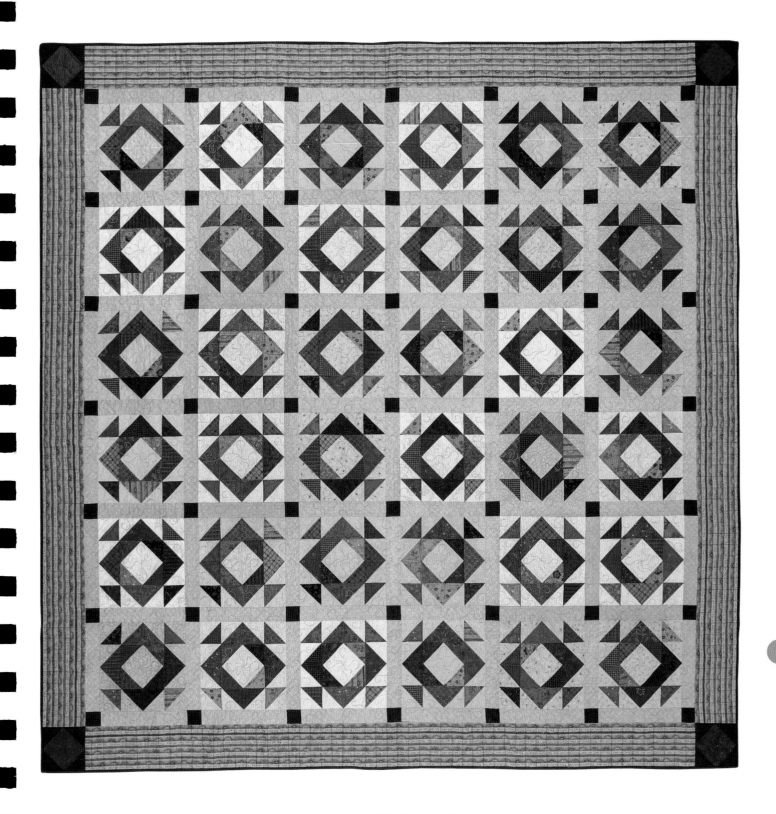

7. Join border corners to ends of remaining border strips; press seams toward border strips. Sew pieced border strips to remaining edges of quilt center to complete quilt top.

Finish Quilt

1. Layer quilt top, batting, and backing; baste. (For details, see Complete the Quilt, *page 159.)* Quilt as desired.

2. Bind with navy blue print binding strips. (For details, see Complete the Quilt.)

EVERYDAY PLACE MATS

Flying Geese blocks in neutral fabrics combine to make

place mats that complement any decor.

Materials

2 yards total assorted cream prints
(blocks, border)

⅝ yard light cream print (binding)

1 yard backing fabric

4—17×21" batting pieces

Finished place mats: 12½×16½"

Cut Fabrics

Cut pieces in the following order.

From assorted cream prints, cut:
• 8—2½×12½" border strips
• 32—3½×6½" rectangles
• 64—3½" squares

From light cream print, cut:
• 7—2½×42" binding strips

From backing fabric, cut:
• 4—17×21" backing rectangles

Assemble and Finish Place Mats

1. Referring to Assemble Flying Geese Units, *page 75*, use assorted cream print 3½×6½" rectangles and 3½" squares to make 32 Flying Geese units.

2. Referring to photo *above right*, lay out eight Flying Geese units in four pairs. Join units in each pair; press seams in one direction. Sew together pairs in each row; press seams in opposite directions. Join rows to make a place mat center. Press seam in one direction.

3. Add assorted cream print 2½×12½" border strips to opposite edges of place mat center to make a place mat top. Press seams toward border.

4. Layer place mat top with 17×21" rectangles of batting and backing; baste. (For details, see Complete the Quilt, *page 159*.)

5. Quilt as desired. The featured place mats are machine-quilted with an allover flame design in each place mat center and a wave pattern in the border.

6. Bind quilted place mat with light cream print binding strips. (For details, see Complete the Quilt.)

7. Repeat steps 2 through 6 to make four place mats total.

ALI'S Quilt

When quiltmaker Shirley Delph decided to create a quilt for her first grandchild, Ali Schippel, she wanted to incorporate scraps of fabrics saved from clothing she'd made for Ali's mom, Robin, when Robin was a baby.

Materials

1⅓ yards muslin (hexagons, Nine-Patch blocks)

¾ yard total assorted prints (Nine-Patch blocks)

⅝ yard total assorted solids (setting triangles)

1¼ yards solid turquoise (border)

5½ yards total jumbo rickrack in assorted colors

1⅓ yards backing fabric

42×46" batting

Finished quilt: 36×40"

Quantities are for 44/45"-wide, 100% cotton fabrics. Measurements include ¼" seam allowances. Sew with right sides together unless otherwise stated.

Cut Fabrics

Cut pieces in the following order. Patterns are on *Pattern Sheet 2*. To make pattern templates, see Cutting with Templates, *page 153*. Border strip measurements allow extra length for mitering corners.

From muslin, cut:
- 284—1½" squares
- 18 of Pattern A
- 4 of Pattern B

From assorted prints, cut:
- 71 sets of five 1½" squares

From assorted solids, cut:
- 54 of Pattern C

From solid turquoise, cut:
- 2—4½×42" border strips
- 2—4½×40" border strips

Assemble Nine-Patch Blocks

Referring to **Diagram 1**, lay out five matching print 1½" squares and four muslin 1½" squares in three rows. Sew together squares in each row. Press seams toward print squares. Join rows to make a Nine-Patch block. Press seams in one direction. The block should be 3½" square including seam allowances. Repeat to make 71 Nine-Patch blocks total.

Diagram 1

continued

Assemble Units

1. Making sure not to sew into the ¼" seam allowances at each end, sew a solid C triangle to one edge of a Nine-Patch block (**Diagram 2**). Press seam toward triangle.

Diagram 2

2. Sew the Step 1 unit to one edge of a muslin A hexagon (**Diagram 3**). Do not sew into seam allowances.

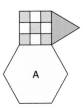

Diagram 3

3. Repeat steps 1 and 2 to add five more Nine-Patch blocks and five more solid C triangles to hexagon, setting in seams as necessary, to make a 6-block unit (**Diagram 4**). (For details, see Setting In Pieces, *page 155*.)

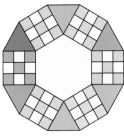

Diagram 4

4. Repeat steps 1 through 3 to make six 6-block units total.

5. In same manner as for 6-block unit, join five Nine-Patch blocks and four assorted solid C triangles to a muslin A hexagon to make a 5-block unit (**Diagram 5**). Repeat to make three 5-block units total.

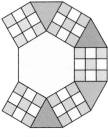
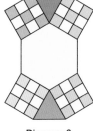

Diagram 5   Diagram 6

6. In same manner as for the 6-block unit, add four Nine-Patch blocks and two assorted solid C triangles to a muslin A hexagon to make a 4-block unit (**Diagram 6**). Repeat to make three 4-block units total.

Assemble Quilt Center

1. Lay out units, muslin A and B pieces, and remaining Nine-Patch blocks in five horizontal rows (**Quilt Assembly Diagram**).

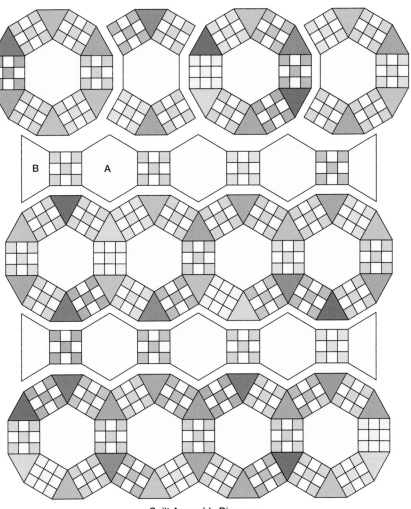

Quilt Assembly Diagram

Ali's Quilt

2. Sew together muslin A and B pieces and Nine-Patch blocks in each sashing row, being careful not to stitch into seam allowances. Press seams toward muslin pieces.

3. Sew together units in each remaining row, setting in seams as necessary. Join rows, setting in seams, to make quilt center. Press seams toward sashing.

Add Border

1. Press under ¼" seam allowance on one long edge of quilt center.

2. With right sides up, position and pin a solid turquoise 4½×42" border strip under pressed edge of quilt center so that raw inside edge of border strip extends ¼" past folded edges of the muslin B pieces **(Diagram 7)**. Position and pin lengths of jumbo rickrack between the two layers, leaving long ends loose at each end of border, and tucking raw ends of rickrack under quilt center edge when changing colors of rickrack.

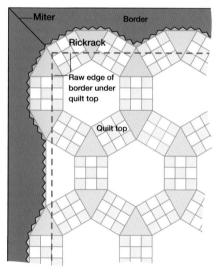

Diagram 7

3. Stitch along edge of quilt center to join the three layers.

4. Press under ¼" seam allowance on adjacent edge of quilt center.

5. Position and pin a solid turquoise 4½×40" border strip in place as before, mitering corners. (For details, see Mitered Border Corners, *page 156*.)

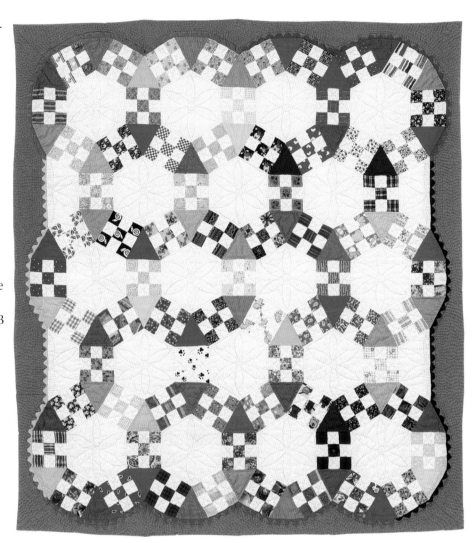

6. Pin rickrack between layers as before, and edgestitch layers together.

7. Repeat steps 1 through 6, adding remaining border strips and rickrack and mitering border corners, to complete quilt top.

Finish Quilt

1. Layer quilt top, batting, and backing; baste. (For details, see Complete the Quilt, *page 159.*)

2. Quilt as desired, leaving outer edges of border unquilted.

3. Trim batting and backing so quilt top is 1¼" larger on all sides. Fold raw edges of border under ¼". Fold border around to the back, mitering corners. Slip-stitch border to backing. Quilt remainder of border as desired.

Ali's Quilt

GARDEN SPLASH WALL HANGING

Batik prints arranged in flower-garden fashion make this wall hanging sparkle.

Materials

1⅔ yards total assorted pink, green, blue, purple, and aqua batiks

¼ yard pink batik (inner border)

⅝ yard multicolor batik (outer border)

⅜ yard navy batik (binding)

1½ yards backing fabric

39×54" batting

Finished quilt: 32½×47½"

Cut Fabrics

Cut pieces in the following order. Use the **Quilt Assembly Diagram** to guide your choices. If possible, arrange pieces on a design wall as you cut them out.

From assorted pink, green, blue, purple, and aqua batiks, cut:
• 936—1½" squares
From pink batik, cut:
• 2—1½×41½" inner border strips
• 2—1½×24½" inner border strips
From multicolor batik, cut:
• 2—3½×41½" outer border strips
• 2—3½×32½" outer border strips
From navy batik, cut:
• 5—2½×42" binding strips

Assemble Blocks

Referring to Assemble Nine-Patch Blocks on *page 82*, use assorted pink, green, blue, purple, and aqua batiks to make a Nine-Patch block. Refer to **Quilt Assembly Diagram** for color placement. Repeat to make 104 Nine-Patch blocks total.

Assemble Quilt Center

1. Lay out blocks in 13 horizontal rows (**Quilt Assembly Diagram**).

2. Sew together blocks in each row. Press seams in one direction, alternating direction with each row. Join rows to make quilt center. Press seams in one direction. The quilt center should be 24½×39½" including seam allowances.

Add Borders

1. Sew short pink batik inner border strips to short

Quilt Assembly Diagram

edges of quilt center. Add long pink batik inner border strips to remaining edges. Press all seams toward inner border.

2. Sew long multicolor batik outer border strips to long edges of quilt center. Add short multicolor batik outer border strips to remaining edges to complete quilt top. Press all seams toward outer border.

Finish Quilt

1. Layer quilt top, batting, and backing; baste. (For details, see Complete the Quilt, *page 159*.)

2. Quilt as desired. The featured project is machine-quilted with a feather design in the center and straight lines on the border.

3. Bind with navy batik binding strips. (For details, see Complete the Quilt.)

RETRO THROW

Lime greens and chocolate browns combine to make this funky throw.

Materials

- 4¾ yards total assorted green and brown prints (blocks)
- ½ yard mottled green (inner border)
- 1 yard brown floral (outer border)
- ⅝ yard dark brown print (binding)
- 3⅔ yards backing fabric
- 66×81" batting

Finished quilt: 59½×74½"

Cut Fabrics

Cut pieces in the following order. This project uses "Ali's Quilt" Pattern B on *Pattern Sheet 2*.

From assorted green and brown prints, cut:
- 264 of Pattern B

From mottled green, cut:
- 6—2×42" strips for inner border

From brown floral, cut:
- 7—4½×42" strips for outer border

From dark brown print, cut:
- 7—2½×42" binding strips

Assemble Quilt Center

1. Referring to photo *opposite*, lay out assorted green and brown print B pieces in 24 rows; when desired, match fabrics in neighboring B pieces to make hexagons.

2. Sew together pieces in each row. Press seams in one direction, alternating direction with each row. Join rows. Press seams in one direction. Trim quilt center to 48½×63½" including seam allowances to complete quilt center.

Add Borders

1. Cut and piece mottled green 2×42" strips to make:
- 2—2×66½" inner border strips
- 2—2×48½" inner border strips

2. Sew short inner border strips to short edges of quilt center. Add long inner border strips to remaining edges. Press all seams toward inner border.

3. Cut and piece brown floral 4½×42" strips to make:
- 2—4½×74½" outer border strips
- 2—4½×51½" outer border strips

4. Add short outer border strips to short edges of quilt center. Join long outer border strips to remaining edges to complete quilt top. Press all seams toward outer border.

Finish Quilt

1. Layer quilt top, batting, and backing; baste. (For details, see Complete the Quilt, *page 159*.)

2. Quilt as desired. Machine-quilter Mary Pepper stitched an allover swirling floral pattern across the quilt top.

3. Bind with dark brown print binding strips. (For details, see Complete the Quilt.)

ROTARY RIOT

The invention of the rotary cutter revolutionized the world of quilting. Now, even the beginning quilter can achieve great accuracy and speed using this simple tool. Throughout the following projects, from the stars in "Sweet Peas" to the scrappy squares in "Trail Mix," novice and experienced quilters alike will delight in the timesaving merits of rotary cutting.

SWEET *Peas*

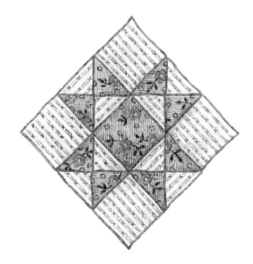

Simple piecing and basic embroidery stitches combine in this lovely

wall hanging from designer Cindy Blackberg.

Materials

1¾ yards ecru print (sashing, border, binding)

⅓ yard pink print (setting and corner triangles)

13—12" squares assorted light prints (blocks)

13—10" squares assorted gold, green, blue,

   and rose prints (blocks)

2½ yards backing fabric

45" square batting

Fine-point permanent marking pen: brown

Perle cotton No. 5: variegated

Finished quilt: 38⅝" square
Finished block: 6" square

Quantities are for 44/45"-wide, 100% cotton fabrics. Measurements include ¼" seam allowances. Sew with right sides together unless otherwise stated.

Designer Notes

Gayle Breska, sister of designer Cindy Blackberg, did the embroidery with variegated perle cotton, devising the design as she went along.

   She first embroidered the sashing and border with a stem-stitched vine, then added flowers, stems, and French knots.

Cut Fabrics

Cut pieces in the following order. Cut sashing strips, border strips, and binding strips lengthwise (parallel to the selvage).

From ecru print, cut:
• 2—2½×42½" sashing strips
• 4—2½×42" binding strips
• 4—2½×40" border strips
• 2—2½×26½" sashing strips
• 2—2½×10½" sashing strips
• 18—2½×6½" sashing rectangles

From pink print, cut:
• 2—9¾" squares, cutting each diagonally twice in an X for 8 setting triangles total
• 2—5⅛" squares, cutting each in half diagonally for 4 corner triangles total

Cut and Assemble Star Blocks

The following instructions result in one star block. Repeat cutting and assembly instructions to make 13 star blocks total.

From one assorted light print, cut:
• 2—3¼" squares
• 4—2½" squares

From one assorted gold, green, blue, or rose print, cut:
• 2—3¼" squares
• 1—2½" square

continued

1. Use a pencil to mark a diagonal line in both directions on wrong side of light print 3¼" squares.

2. Layer each marked light print 3¼" square atop a gold, green, blue, or rose print 3¼" square. Sew together each pair with two seams, stitching ¼" on each side of one drawn line (**Diagram 1**).

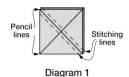

Pencil lines — Stitching lines

Diagram 1

3. Referring to **Diagram 2**, cut a stitched pair apart on both drawn lines to make four triangle units. Repeat with second stitched pair to make eight triangle units total. Press triangle units open, pressing seams toward darker print, to make pieced triangles.

Diagram 2

4. Sew together two pieced triangles to make an hourglass unit (**Diagram 3**). Press seam open.

The unit should be 2½" square including seam allowances. Repeat to make four hourglass units total.

Diagram 3

5. Referring to **Diagram 4**, lay out four light print 2½" squares; four hourglass units; and one gold, green, blue, or rose print 2½" square in rows. Sew together pieces in each row. Press seams away from hourglass units. Join rows to make a star block. Press seams in one direction. The star block should be 6½" square including seam allowances.

Diagram 4

Assemble Quilt Center

1. Referring to **Quilt Assembly Diagram**, lay out star blocks, sashing rectangles, sashing strips, and setting triangles in diagonal rows.

2. Sew together pieces in each block row. Press seams toward sashing rectangles. Then join block rows and sashing strips. Press seams in one direction. Add four pink print corner triangles to complete quilt center. Press seams toward corner triangles.

3. Trim sashing strips even with edges of quilt center. The quilt center should be 34⅝" square including seam allowances.

Add Border

With midpoints aligned, sew ecru print 2½×40" border strips to opposite edges of quilt center, beginning and ending seams ¼" from corners. Add remaining ecru print 2½×40" border strips, mitering corners, to complete quilt top. (For details, see Mitered Border Corners, *page 156*.) Press seams toward border.

Embroider Quilt Top

The Full-Size Embroidery Pattern is on *Pattern Sheet 2*. All embroidery is done with one length of variegated perle cotton.

Sweet Peas

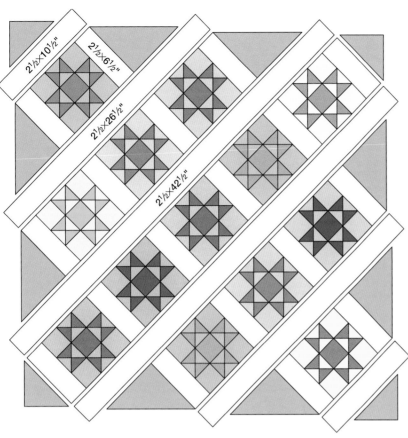

2½x10½"
2½x6½"
2½x26½"
2½x42½"

Quilt Assembly Diagram

1. Referring to **Embroidery Diagram**, use a light table and a brown fine-point permanent marking pen to trace Embroidery Pattern onto sashing and border, using tiny dots to indicate French knots.

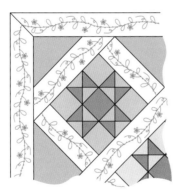

Embroidery Diagram

2. Stem-stitch the vine. To stem-stitch, pull your needle up at A **(Stem Stitch Diagram)**. Insert your needle back into fabric at B, about ¼" away from A. Holding thread out of the way, bring your needle back up at C and pull thread through so it lies flat against fabric. Distances between points A, B, and C should be equal. Pull with equal tautness after each stitch.

3. Referring to **Embroidery Diagram**, embellish stem-stitched vine with flowers made of couched lazy daisy stitches, and stems and leaves made of stem stitches. Make French knots in flower centers and where indicated along vine.

To make a couched lazy daisy stitch, pull your needle up at A **(Couched Lazy Daisy Stitch Diagram)**, leaving a loop on fabric surface. Insert your needle back into fabric at B, about ¹⁄₁₆" away from A. Bring your needle up at C and gently pull your needle and trailing thread until loop lies flat against fabric. Push your needle through to back at D and come up at E. Insert your needle back down at F to secure one side of loop. Come up at G and go back down at H to secure other side of loop.

To make a French knot, pull your needle up at A **(French Knot Diagram)**, the point where the knot is desired. Wrap thread around your needle twice without twisting it. Insert tip of needle into fabric at B, ¹⁄₁₆" away from A. Gently push wraps down needle to meet fabric. Pull your needle and trailing thread through fabric slowly and smoothly.

Finish Quilt

1. Layer quilt top, batting, and backing; baste. (For details, see Complete the Quilt, *page 159.*)

2. Quilt as desired. On the featured quilt, Cindy hand-quilted a one-inch grid across the quilt top and straight lines in the border.

3. Bind with ecru print binding strips. (For details, see Complete the Quilt.)

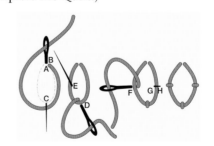

Couched Lazy Daisy Stitch

Stem Stitch

French Knot

SPARKLING STARS TABLE TOPPER

Jewel-tone stars sparkle on this striking accent piece.

Materials

I yard dark gold print (setting squares, setting and
corner triangles)

I yard total assorted pink, blue, green, purple,
orange, and red prints (blocks)

I yard mottled cream (blocks)

¾ yard green print (border)

½ yard navy print (binding)

2¾ yards backing fabric

49×57" batting

Finished quilt: 42½×51"

Cut Fabrics

Cut pieces in the following order.

From dark gold print, cut:
• 4—9¾" squares, cutting each diagonally twice
in an X for 16 setting triangles total (you will
use 14)
• 12—6½" squares
• 2—5⅛" squares, cutting each in half diagonally
for 4 corner triangles total
From green print, cut:
• 5—4½×42" strips for border
From navy print, cut:
• 5—2½×42" binding strips

Assemble Blocks

Referring to Cut and Assemble Star Blocks, *page 93*,
use assorted pink, blue, green, purple, orange,
and red prints and mottled cream to make 20 star
blocks total.

Assemble Quilt Center

1. Referring to photo at *left*, lay out 20 star blocks,
12 dark gold print 6½" setting squares, and 14 gold
print setting triangles in diagonal rows.

2. Sew together pieces in each row. Press seams
toward dark gold print. Join rows. Press seams
in one direction. Add gold print corner triangles
to make quilt center. The quilt center should be
34½×43" including seam allowances.

Add Border

1. Cut and piece green print 4½×42" strips to make:
• 2—4½×43" border strips
• 2—4½×42½" border strips

2. Sew long border strips to long edges of quilt
center. Add short border strips to remaining edges
to complete quilt top. Press seams toward border.

Finish Quilt

1. Layer quilt top, batting, and backing; baste.
(For details, see Complete the Quilt, *page 159*.)

2. Quilt as desired. Machine-quilter Susan Urich stitched a diagonal grid across the quilt center and a cable design in the border.

3. Bind with navy print binding strips. (For details, see Complete the Quilt.)

SWEET PILLOW

Soft colors and simple embroidery highlight this delicate little pillow.

Materials

8×12" piece *each* pink, green, and blue prints
   (hourglass units)

½ yard white-on-white print (hourglass units,
   border, pillow back)

5" square *each* pink, green, and blue plaids (border)

Embroidery floss: pink, green, blue

12×16" pillow form

Finished pillow: 16×12"

Cut Fabrics

Cut pieces in the following order. This project uses "Sweet Peas" Full-Size Embroidery Pattern on *Pattern Sheet 2*.

From *each* pink, green, and blue print, cut:
• 5—3¼" squares
From white-on-white print, cut:
• 1—12½×16½" rectangle
• 1—2½×12½" rectangle
• 15—3¼" squares
From *each* pink, green, and blue plaid, cut:
• 1—4½" square

Assemble Pillow Top

1. Referring to Cut and Assemble Star Blocks, *page 93*, steps 1 through 4, use pink, green, and blue print 3¼" squares and white-on-white print 3¼" squares to make 30 hourglass units total.

2. Referring to **Pillow Assembly Diagram**, lay out hourglass units in six rows. Sew together pieces in each row. Press seams in one direction, alternating direction with each row. Join rows to make hourglass section. Press seams in one direction.

3. Lay out pink, green, and blue plaid 4½" squares in a vertical row. Sew together to make plaid row. Press seams in one direction. Align white-on-white print 2½×12½" rectangle with long edge of plaid row. Sew together to make a border unit; press seam toward rectangle.

4. Referring to **Pillow Assembly Diagram**, join border unit with hourglass section to make pillow top. Press seam toward border unit. The pillow top should be 12½×16½" including seam allowances.

5. Referring to Embroider Quilt Top, *page 94*, use six strands of pink floss for lazy daisy flowers, green floss for couched lazy daisy leaves and stem-stitch vines, and blue floss for French knot buds and flower centers to embellish white-on-white print section of border.

Finish Pillow

1. Layer pillow top and white-on-white print 12½×16½" pillow back rectangle. Stitch around edges, leaving an opening on one short edge to insert pillow form.

2. Turn pillow cover right side out and insert pillow form. Whipstitch opening closed to complete pillow.

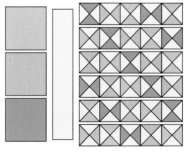

Pillow Assembly Diagram

BOSTON
Commons

Quiltmaker Darlene Zimmerman used scraps of reproduction fabrics that she designed and the traditional Boston Commons pattern to create a cheerful bed-size quilt with a nostalgic look. She varied the design by laying out the squares in rows rather than in the usual concentric arrangement.

Materials

3¾ yards total assorted 1930s reproduction prints (rows)

3⅝ yards solid yellow (rows, sashing, binding)

4¼ yards backing fabric

75×83" batting

Finished quilt: 68½×76⅞"

Quantities are for 44/45"-wide, 100% cotton fabrics. Measurements include ¼" seam allowances. Sew with right sides together unless otherwise stated.

Cut Fabrics

Cut pieces in the following order. Cut sashing and binding strips lengthwise (parallel to the selvage).

From assorted 1930s reproduction prints, cut:
- 154—2½×10½" strips
- 114—2½" squares

From solid yellow, cut:
- 3—4¼×65⅝" sashing strips
- 2—3⅜×65⅝" sashing strips
- 5—2½×65" binding strips
- 2—3⅜×62¾" sashing strips
- 97—4⅛" squares, cutting each diagonally twice in an X for 388 large triangles total
- 16—2⅜" squares, cutting each in half diagonally for 32 small triangles total

Assemble Pieced Strips

1. Referring to **Diagram 1**, join four reproduction print 2½×10½" strips to make Strip Set A. Press seams in one direction. Repeat to make 22 total of Strip Set A.

2. Cut A strip sets into a total of eighty-eight 2½"-wide A segments.

3. Referring to **Diagram 2**, join three reproduction print 2½×10½" strips to make Strip Set B. Press seams in one direction. Repeat to make 22 total of Strip Set B.

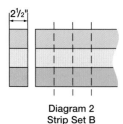

Diagram 1
Strip Set A

Diagram 2
Strip Set B

continued

4. Cut B strip sets into a total of eighty-eight 2½"-wide B segments.

5. Join an A segment and a B segment to make a pieced strip (**Diagram 3**). Press seam to one side. Repeat to make 80 pieced strips total.

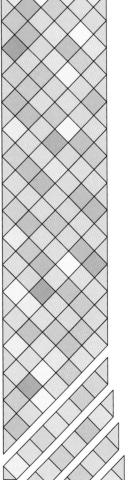

Diagram 3

Assemble Pieced Units

1. Referring to **Diagram 4**, sew solid yellow large triangles to opposite edges of a reproduction print 2½" square. Press seams toward triangles. Add a solid yellow small triangle to make Unit A. Repeat to make eight total of Unit A.

Diagram 4
Unit A

2. Referring to **Diagram 5**, sew together one Strip Set B segment and two solid yellow large triangles in a row to make Unit B. Press seams in one direction. Repeat to make eight total of Unit B.

Diagram 5
Unit B

3. Join one Strip Set A segment, one reproduction print 2½" square, and two solid yellow large triangles in a row to make Unit C (**Diagram 6**). Press seams in one direction. Repeat to make eight total of Unit C.

Diagram 6
Unit C

4. Referring to **Diagram 7**, sew together one pieced strip, one solid yellow large triangle, and one solid yellow small triangle in a row to make Unit D. Press seams in one direction. Repeat to make eight total of Unit D.

Diagram 7
Unit D

5. Join one pieced strip and two solid yellow large triangles in a row to make Unit E (**Diagram 8**). Press seams in one direction. Repeat to make 72 total of Unit E.

Diagram 8
Unit E

Assemble Quilt Center

1. Referring to **Diagram 9**, lay out two *each* of units A, B, C, and D, and 18 of Unit E in a vertical row.

2. Sew together units in row. Handle pieces carefully to avoid distortion. Press seams in one direction. The row should be 11⅞×65⅝" including seam allowances.

3. Repeat steps 1 and 2 to make four pieced rows total. Referring to photo *opposite*, lay out the four pieced rows, three solid yellow 4¼×65⅝" sashing strips, and two solid yellow 3⅜×65⅝" sashing strips. Sew together; press seams toward sashing. Add solid yellow 3⅜×62¾" sashing strips to remaining edges to complete quilt center. Press seams toward sashing. The quilt center should be 62¾×71¼" including seam allowances.

Assemble and Add Border

1. Sew solid yellow large triangles to opposite edges of a reproduction print 2½" square (**Diagram 10**) to make a Unit 1. Press seams toward solid yellow triangles. Repeat to make 90 total of Unit 1.

2. Referring to **Diagram 11**, join a solid yellow large triangle and solid yellow small triangle to opposite edges of a reproduction print 2½" square; press seams toward triangles. Add a second solid yellow small triangle to make a Unit 2. Press seam toward triangle. Repeat to make eight total of Unit 2.

Diagram 9

Diagram 10

Diagram 11

3. Carefully matching seams, join 20 of Unit 1 and two of Unit 2 in a row to make a short border strip (**Diagram 12**). Press seams in one direction. The short border strip should be 3⅜×62¾" including seam allowances. Repeat to make a second short border strip. Sew short border strips to short edges of quilt center. Press seams toward sashing.

4. Join 25 of Unit 1 and two of Unit 2 to make a long border strip. Press seams in one direction. The long border strip should be 3⅜×76⅞" including seam allowances. Repeat to make a second long

border strip. Sew long border strips to remaining edges of quilt center to complete quilt top. Press seams toward sashing.

Finish Quilt
1. Layer quilt top, batting, and backing; baste. (For details, see Complete the Quilt, *page 159.*) Quilt as desired.

2. Bind with solid yellow binding strips. (For details, see Complete the Quilt.)

Diagram 12

continued

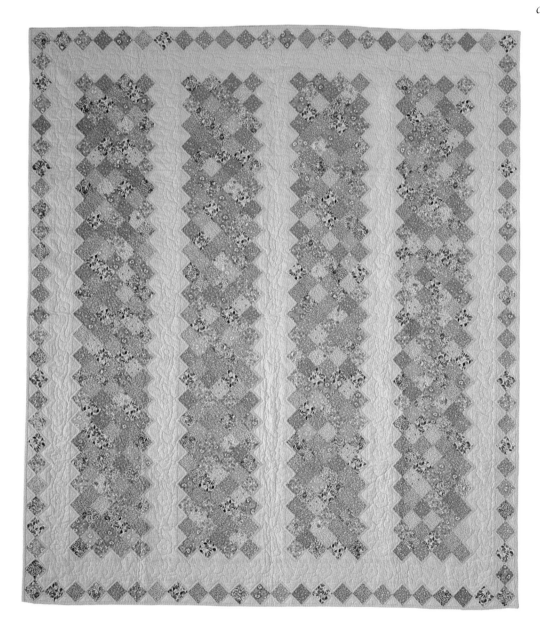

optional colors

Dramatic Changes

Quilt tester Laura Boehnke pushed her creative talents to the edge with this dynamic rendition of "Boston Commons."

Using a graphic collection of fabrics, Laura carefully placed a row of red squares in the middle, surrounded by black, then white. The red print border adds even more drama.

COLOR IT YOUR OWN

Color is often the first thing that attracts us to a quilt. It makes a statement about the quiltmaker and expresses an overall mood of the quilt. Use the following illustrations as a color springboard when designing your next quilt project.

Creating a quilt that reflects who you are starts with color choice. The easiest way to select colors is to choose what you like. Keep in mind contrast, value, and variety of print sizes and styles when defining the look of your quilt. High contrast, as in the example *below left*, creates the greatest visual tension. Quilts with a black background tend to be bright and exciting. Colors that are less vibrant, as in the design *below right*, result in a more blended and restful design.

Changing the fabric placement in a design will expand the focus from the quilt center to the border, as in the blue-and-gray example *below, top left.* Color also can express a theme, such as a '30s-era or baby quilt with vintage or pastel prints *below, bottom left and right.* Monochromatic schemes, as in the red design *below, top right,* create natural shading. Be playful with color and let your imagination soar—the possibilities are endless.

SHEET SET

Set the mood for a restful yet stylish bedroom with sheets

bordered in a sophisticated design.

Materials

¼ yard *each* aqua and cream prints (squares)

¾ yard brown print (triangles)

Queen-size flat sheet (90×102")

Two queen-size pillowcases (20×30")

Cut Fabrics

Cut pieces in the following order. If your sheet set measurements vary from those listed *above,* adjust the number of squares and triangles as needed to fit the sheet and pillowcases.

From aqua print, cut:
• 32—2½" squares
From cream print, cut:
• 30—2½" squares
From brown print, cut:
• 30—4⅛" squares, cutting each diagonally twice in an X for 120 large triangles total (you will use 118 large triangles)
• 6—2⅜" squares, cutting each in half diagonally for 12 small triangles total

Assemble and Add Pieced Borders

1. Referring to Assemble and Add Border, *page 102,* steps 1 through 3, use 16 aqua print 2½" squares, 16 cream print 2½" squares, 62 brown print large triangles, and four brown print small triangles to make a top sheet border strip.

2. Referring to **Border Placement Diagram**, center border strip on flat sheet header 2½" from hemmed edge. Trim both ends of border strip ¼" beyond finished edges of flat sheet. Press under a ¼" hem on all edges of border. Reposition border on sheet and generously pin in place. Using matching thread, topstitch border to flat sheet header.

3. Using eight aqua print 2½" squares, seven cream print 2½" squares, 28 brown print large triangles, and four brown print small triangles, repeat Step 1 to make a pillowcase border. Repeat to make a second pillowcase border. Press under ¼" hem, position, and topstitch in the same manner as for the flat sheet.

Border Placement Diagram

TRAIL *Mix*

If you've got a stash of fabric scraps, designer Mabeth Oxenreider

has the perfect project for you to put them to good use.

Materials

½ yard purple print (inner border)

⅔ yard gold print (middle border, piping)

2¼ yards green print (outer border, binding)

8 yards total assorted light, medium, and

    dark prints (blocks)

7½ yards backing fabric

90×108" batting

Finished quilt: 84×102"
Finished blocks: 6" square

Quantities are for 44/45"-wide, 100% cotton fabrics. Measurements include ¼" seam allowances. Sew with right sides together unless otherwise stated.

Designer Notes

While the piecing of this quilt top is relatively simple, gathering a variety of fabric scraps, such as designer Mabeth Oxenreider used to make the photographed quilt, could take awhile. That's why the yardage requirement for the blocks is specified as a total amount (see Materials) rather than being identified by fabric color.

Mabeth chose prints with varieties of texture, value, and scale, and she used light shirtings in the Triple Four-Patch blocks. She also found that reproduction fabrics work well. She suggests avoiding tone-on-tone prints, as they appear solid from a distance.

Mabeth pieced 180 blocks in five different patterns to compose this quilt. If you want to make a less scrappy version, strip piecing may simplify the construction (see *page 110*).

Cut Fabrics

Cut border, piping, and binding pieces in the following order. Cutting instructions for individual blocks follow in each section.

From purple print, cut:
• 9—1½×42" strips for inner border
From gold print, cut:
• 9—1¼×42" strips for middle border
• 10—¾×42" strips for piping
From green print, cut:
• 10—4½×42" strips for outer border
• 10—2½×42" binding strips

Cut and Assemble Four-Patch Blocks

From assorted prints, cut:
• 4—3½" squares

1. Referring to **Diagram 1** on *page 110*, sew together squares in pairs. Press seams in opposite directions. Sew together pairs to make

continued

a Four-Patch block. Press seam in one direction. The block should be 6½" square including seam allowances.

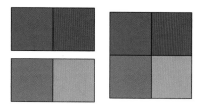

Diagram 1

2. Repeat cutting instructions and Step 1 to make 32 Four-Patch blocks total.

Cut and Assemble Double Four-Patch Blocks

From assorted prints, cut:
• 2—3½" squares
• 8—2" squares

1. Join four 2" squares in pairs (**Diagram 2**). Press seams in opposite directions. Sew together pairs to make a Four-Patch unit. Press seam in one direction. The unit should be 3½" square including seam allowances. Repeat to make a second Four-Patch unit.

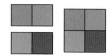

Diagram 2

2. Sew together two 3½" squares and two Four-Patch units in pairs (**Diagram 3**). Press seams toward 3½" squares. Join pairs to make a Double Four-Patch block. Press seam in one direction. The block should be 6½" square including seam allowances.

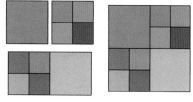

Diagram 3

3. Repeat cutting instructions and steps 1 and 2 to make 38 Double Four-Patch blocks total.

Cut and Assemble Triple Four-Patch Blocks

From one assorted print, cut:
• 2—3½" squares
• 4—2" squares

From one medium or dark print, cut:
• 1—1¼×12" strip

From one light print, cut:
• 1—1¼×12" strip

1. Aligning long edges, sew together the medium or dark print 1¼×12" strip and the light print 1¼×12" strip to make a strip set (**Diagram 4**). Press seam toward darker strip. Cut strip set into eight 1¼"-wide segments.

Diagram 4

2. Sew together two Step 1 segments as shown (**Diagram 5**) to make a Four-Patch unit. The unit should be 2" square including seam allowances. Repeat to make four Four-Patch units total.

Diagram 5

Strip-piecing method: To speed up the cutting and piecing of the Four-Patch units, Mabeth suggests using a strip-piecing technique. After assembling a strip set, cut it in half. Layer the two halves with right sides together, making sure the light strip from one half is atop the dark strip from the other half (**Diagram 6**). Because the seam allowances are pressed toward the dark strip, they're now in opposite directions, causing the two halves to "lock" in place. Cut the layered strip set into 1¼"-wide segments; then sew the layered segments together along one edge to make Four-Patch units. Carefully handle the segments as you move them to the sewing machine so you don't "unlock" the seams.

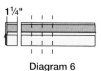

Diagram 6

continued

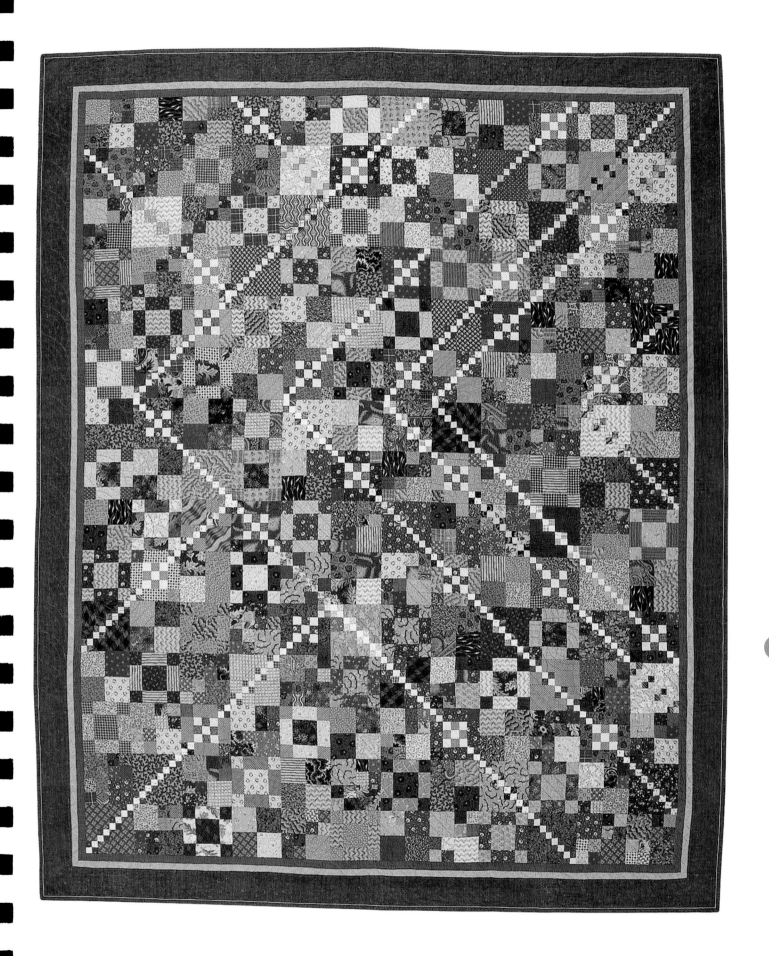

3. Sew together two Four-Patch units and two 2" squares in pairs (**Diagram 7**; note placement of light squares in Four-Patch units). Press seams toward 2" squares. Join pairs to make a Double Four-Patch unit. Press seam in one direction. The unit should be 3½" square including seam allowances. Repeat to make a second Double Four-Patch unit.

Diagram 7

4. Sew together two Double Four-Patch units and two 3½" squares in pairs (**Diagram 8**). Press seams toward 3½" squares. Join pairs to make a Triple Four-Patch block. Press seam in one direction. The block should be 6½" square including seam allowances.

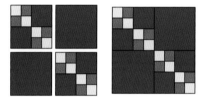

Diagram 8

5. Repeat cutting instructions and steps 1 through 4 to make 44 Triple Four-Patch blocks total.

Cut and Assemble Double Nine-Patch Blocks

From one medium or dark print, cut:
• 4—1½" squares
From *each* of two medium or dark prints and two light prints, cut:
• 2—1¼" squares
From one light print, cut:
• 5—1½" squares
From assorted prints, cut:
• 2—2" squares
From one assorted print, cut:
• 4—2×3½" rectangles

I. Sew together two medium or dark print 1¼" squares and two light print 1¼" squares in pairs. Press seams in opposite directions. Sew together pairs to make a Four-Patch unit (**Diagram 9**). Press seam in one direction. The unit should be 2" square including seam allowances. Repeat to make a second Four-Patch unit.

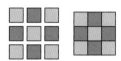

Diagram 9

2. Referring to **Diagram 10**, lay out four medium or dark print 1½" squares and five light print 1½" squares in three rows. Sew together squares in each row. Press seams toward darker squares. Join rows to make a Nine-Patch unit. Press seams in one direction. The unit should be 3½" square including seam allowances.

Diagram 10

3. Referring to **Diagram 11**, lay out two 2" squares, two Four-Patch units, one Nine-Patch unit, and four 2×3½" rectangles in three rows. Sew together pieces in each row. Press seams toward rectangles. Join rows to make a Double Nine-Patch block. Press seams in one direction. The block should be 6½" square including seam allowances.

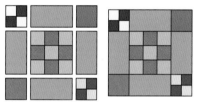

Diagram 11

4. Repeat cutting instructions and steps 1 through 3 to make 24 Double Nine-Patch blocks total.

Cut and Assemble Nine-Patch Blocks

From one assorted print, cut:
• 1—3½" square
• 4—2" squares
From a second assorted print, cut:
• 4—2×3½" rectangles

I. Referring to **Diagram 12**, lay out four 2" squares, the 3½" square, and four 2×3½" rectangles. Sew together pieces in each row. Press seams toward darker pieces. Join rows to make a Nine-Patch block. Press seams in one direction. The block should be 6½" square including seam allowances.

2. Repeat cutting instructions and Step 1 to make 42 Nine-Patch blocks total.

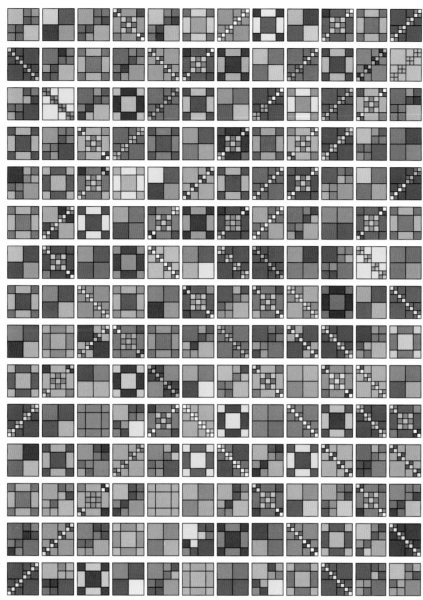

Quilt Assembly Diagram

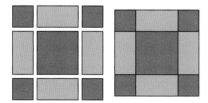

Diagram 12

Assemble Quilt Center

1. Referring to **Quilt Assembly Diagram**, lay out 32 Four-Patch blocks, 38 Double Four-Patch blocks, 44 Triple Four-Patch blocks, 24 Double Nine-Patch blocks, and 42 Nine-Patch blocks in 15 horizontal rows.

2. Sew together blocks in each row. Press seams in one direction, alternating direction with each row. Join rows to make quilt center. Press seams in one direction. The quilt center should be $72\frac{1}{2}\times90\frac{1}{2}$" including seam allowances.

Add Borders

1. Cut and piece purple print $1\frac{1}{2}\times42$" strips to make:
- 2—$1\frac{1}{2}\times92\frac{1}{2}$" inner border strips
- 2—$1\frac{1}{2}\times72\frac{1}{2}$" inner border strips

2. Sew short inner border strips to short edges of quilt center. Join long inner border strips to remaining edges. Press all seams toward inner border.

continued

Trail Mix

3. Cut and piece gold print 1¼×42" strips to make:
• 2—1¼×94" middle border strips
• 2—1¼×74½" middle border strips

4. Sew short middle border strips to short edges of quilt center. Join long middle border strips to remaining edges. Press all seams toward middle border.

5. Cut and piece green print 4½×42" strips to make:
• 2—4½×102" outer border strips
• 2—4½×76" outer border strips

6. Sew short outer border strips to short edges of quilt center. Join long outer border strips to remaining edges to complete quilt top. Press seams toward outer border.

Finish Quilt

1. Layer quilt top, batting, and backing; baste. (For details, see Complete the Quilt, *page 159*.)

2. Quilt as desired. Mabeth machine-quilted parallel lines, cables, and swirls across her quilt top, diagonally orienting her stitches along the same lines as the Triple Four-Patch blocks. She extended her designs onto the borders.

3. Cut and piece gold print ¾×42" strips to make:
• 1—¾×385" piping strip

4. With wrong side inside, fold and press piping strip in half lengthwise to make ⅜"-wide piping.

5. Aligning raw edges and using a ¼" seam, baste piping to quilt top.

6. Bind with green print binding strips. (For details, see Complete the Quilt.) *Note:* About ⅛" of the gold piping will show between quilt top and binding edge once binding is turned back.

optional colors

Happy Trails

"There are so many options to explore with the 'Trail Mix' pattern," quilt tester Laura Boehnke says. "I deliberately placed the Triple Four-Patch blocks on my color option so they'd form a secondary diamond pattern in the quilt center."

Using a variety of Americana prints from her stash, Laura eliminated the piping but kept the original triple border combination to complete her 9×9 block version.

Trail Mix

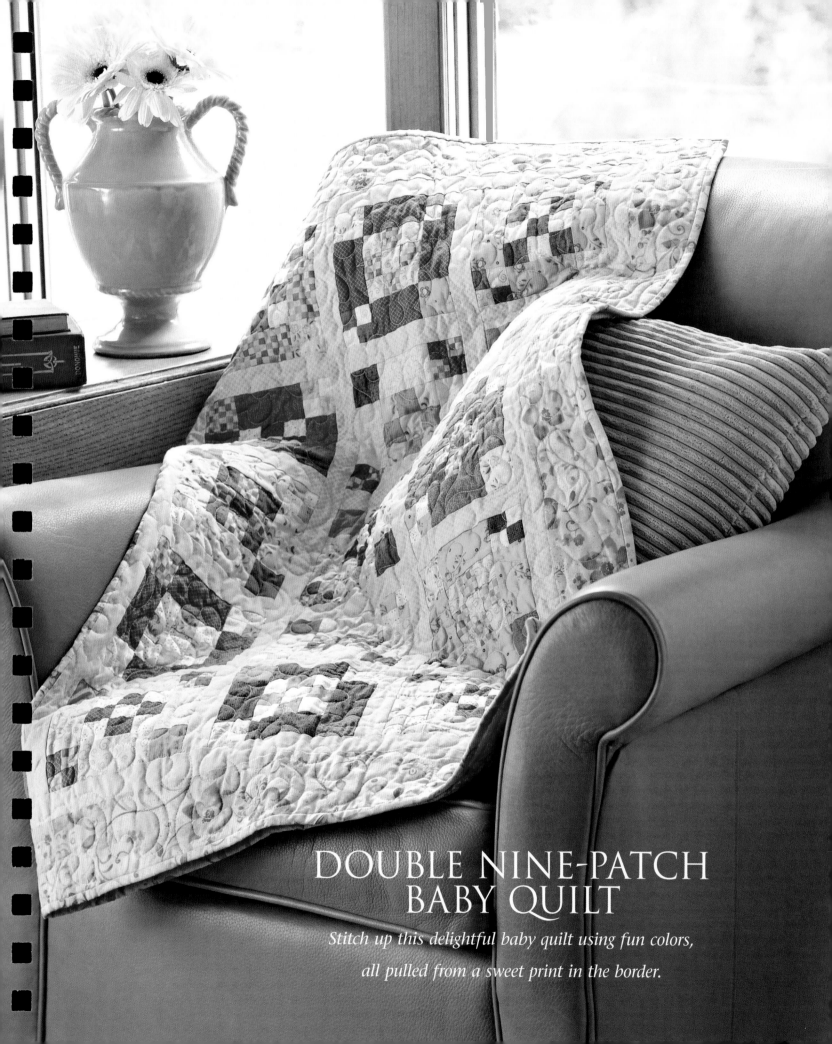

DOUBLE NINE-PATCH
BABY QUILT

Stitch up this delightful baby quilt using fun colors,

all pulled from a sweet print in the border.

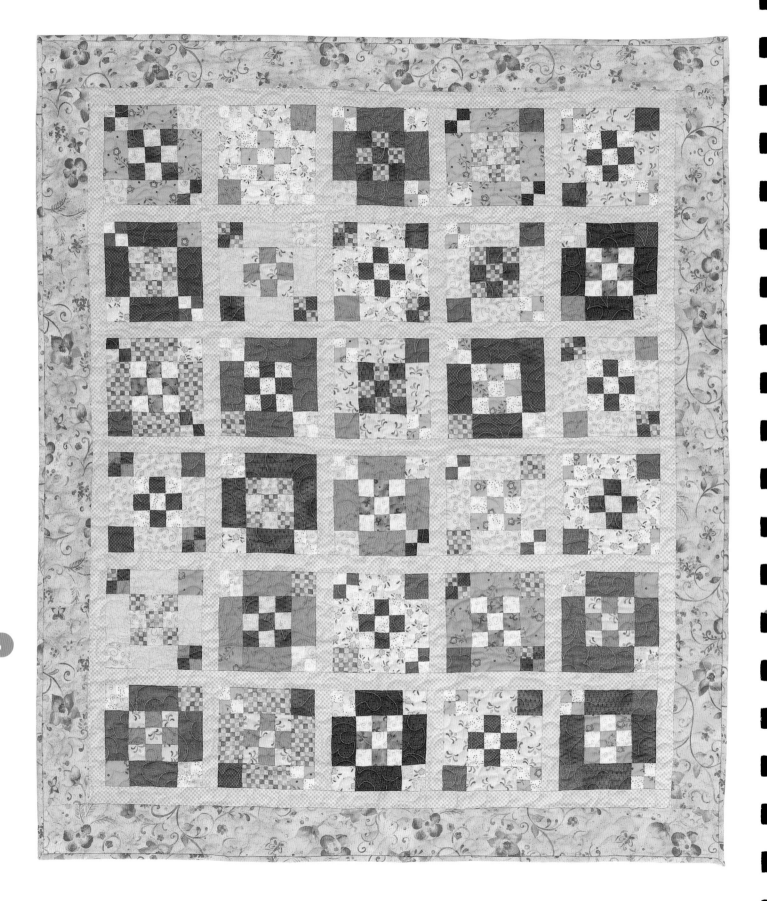

Trail Mix

Materials

⅔ yard light green print (sashing, inner border)

1 yard pink print (outer border, binding)

1⅞ yards total assorted light, medium,
    and dark prints (blocks)

2¾ yards backing fabric

49×56" batting

Finished quilt: 42½×49½"

Cut Fabrics

Cut pieces in the following order.

From light green print, cut:
• 4—1½×42" strips for inner border
• 5—1½×34½" sashing strips
• 24—1½×6½" sashing rectangles
From pink print, cut:
• 5—3½×42" strips for outer border
• 5—2½×42" binding strips

Cut and Assemble Blocks

Referring to Cut and Assemble Double Nine-Patch
Blocks, *page 112*, cutting instructions and steps
1 through 3, use assorted light, medium, and dark
prints to make 30 Double Nine-Patch blocks.

Assemble Quilt Center

1. Referring to **Quilt Assembly Diagram**, lay out
30 Double Nine-Patch blocks, 24 light green print
1½×6½" sashing rectangles, and five light green
print 1½×34½" sashing strips in 11 rows.

2. Join pieces in each block row. Press seams
toward sashing strips. Join rows to make quilt
center. Press seams toward sashing. The quilt
center should be 34½×41½" including seam
allowances.

Add Borders

1. Cut light green print 1½×42" strips to make:
• 2—1½×41½" inner border strips
• 2—1½×36½" inner border strips

2. Sew long inner border strips to long edges
of quilt center. Add short inner border strips to
remaining edges. Press all seams toward border.

3. Cut and piece pink print 3½×42" strips to make:
• 2—3½×43½" outer border strips
• 2—3½×42½" outer border strips

4. Sew long outer border strips to long edges
of quilt center. Add short outer border strips to
remaining edges to complete quilt top. Press seams
toward outer border.

Finish Quilt

1. Layer quilt top, batting, and backing; baste.
(For details, see Complete the Quilt, *page 159*.)

2. Quilt as desired. Machine-quilter Kelly Edwards
stitched a meandering leaf design across the
quilt top.

3. Bind with pink print binding strips. (For details,
see Complete the Quilt.)

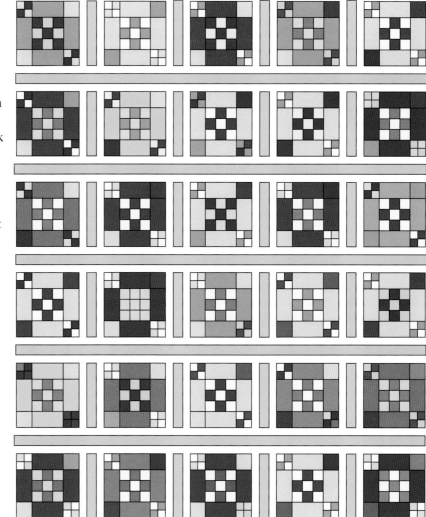

Quilt Assembly Diagram

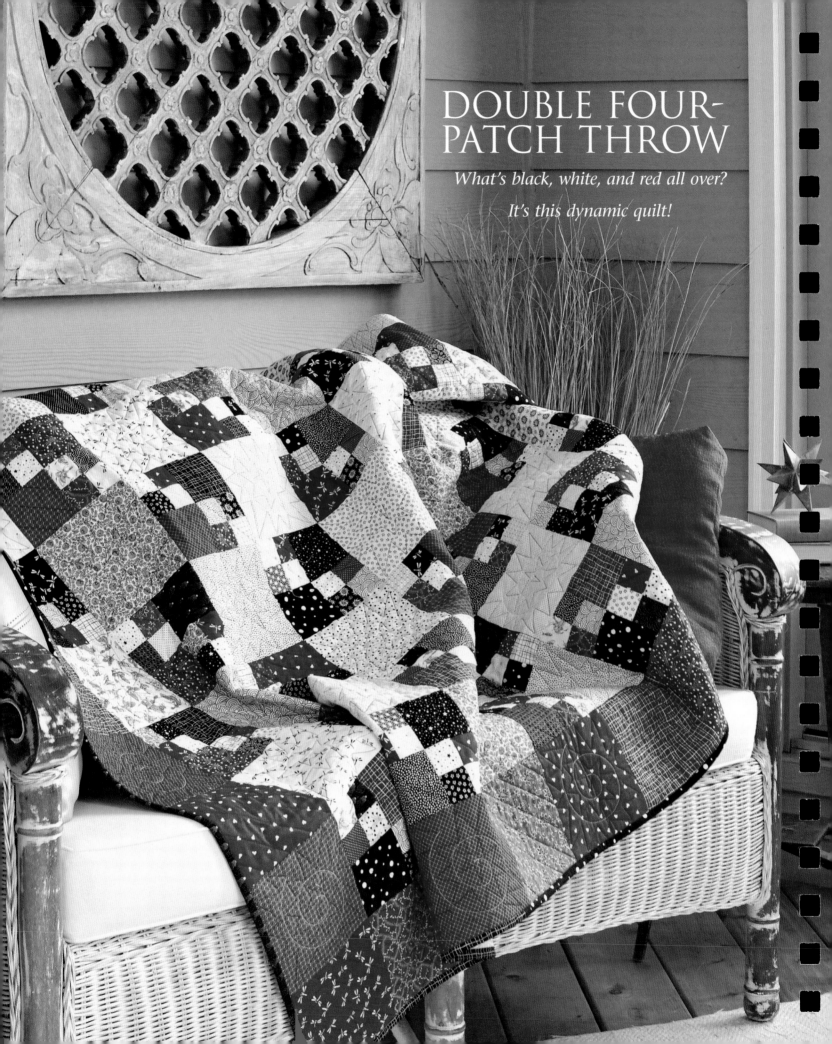

DOUBLE FOUR-PATCH THROW

What's black, white, and red all over?

It's this dynamic quilt!

Materials

1¾ yards total assorted white shirtings
(blocks, setting squares)

1¼ yards total assorted black shirtings
(blocks, binding)

1⅞ yards total assorted red shirtings
(blocks, border)

3½ yards backing fabric

61×73" batting

Finished quilt: 54½×66½"

Cut Fabrics

Cut pieces in the following order.

From assorted white shirtings, cut:
- 31—6½" setting squares
- 128—2" squares

From assorted black shirtings, cut:
- Enough 2½"-wide pieces in lengths ranging from 10" to 20" to total 265" for binding
- 35—3½" squares
- 67—2" squares

From assorted red shirtings, cut:
- 36—6½" squares for border
- 29—3½" squares
- 61—2" squares

Assemble Double Four-Patch Blocks

Referring to **Diagram 13** and Cut and Assemble Double Four-Patch Blocks, *page 110*, steps 1 and 2, use white shirting 2" squares, black shirting 3½" and 2" squares, and red shirting 3½" and 2" squares to make 32 Double Four-Patch blocks.

Diagram 13

Assemble Quilt Top

1. Referring to photo at *right* for placement, lay out 32 Double Four-Patch blocks and 31 white shirting 6½" setting squares in nine rows.

2. Join pieces in each row. Press seams toward setting squares. Join rows to make quilt center. Press seams in one direction. The quilt center should be 42½×54½" including seam allowances.

3. Sew together seven red shirting 6½" squares to make a short border strip. Press seams in one direction. Repeat to make a second short border strip.

4. Join 11 red shirting 6½" squares to make a long border strip. Press seams in one direction. Repeat to make a second long border strip.

5. Sew short border strips to short edges of quilt center. Add long border strips to remaining edges to complete the quilt top. Press seams toward border.

Finish Quilt

1. Layer quilt top, batting, and backing; baste. (For details, see Complete the Quilt, *page 159*.)

2. Quilt as desired. Machine-quilter Susan Urich stitched diagonal lines through the blocks and spiral sunbursts in the setting squares and border.

3. Bind with black shirting binding strips. (For details, see Complete the Quilt.)

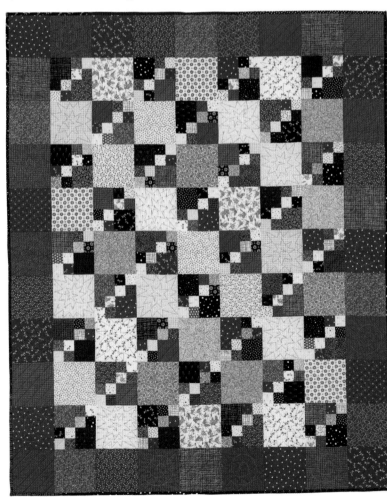

ENCHANTING APPLIQUÉ

Appliqué allows the imagination to soar. Virtually any shape is possible, eliminating many of the limitations encountered in traditional piecing. Appliqué techniques range from hand stitching to fusing and machine work, depending on the quilt's intended use and the quilter's preference. Explore the appliqué projects in this chapter and, if necessary, adapt the methods used to your preferred technique.

OHIO *Memories*

Designer Cheryl Pedersen pieced a background of Ohio Star blocks and appliquéd it with Ohio roses to create a quilt with true regional flavor. The border's redwork verse speaks of friendship.

Materials

- 1¼ yards gold print (blocks, flower center appliqués, inner border)
- 1¾ yards beige print (blocks, outer border)
- 1 yard light beige print (setting squares and triangles, corner triangles)
- 1⅓ yards olive green print (stem and leaf appliqués, binding)
- ⅓ yard red moiré (flower appliqués)
- ¼ yard red print (flower appliqués)
- 3⅛ yards backing fabric
- 56" square batting
- Embroidery floss: red
- Fine-point permanent marking pen: red

Finished quilt: 49¾" square
Finished block: 9" square

Unless otherwise specified, quantities are for 44/45"-wide, 100% cotton fabrics. Measurements include ¼" seam allowances. Sew with right sides together unless otherwise stated.

Cut Fabrics

Cut pieces in the following order. Patterns are on *Pattern Sheet 1*. To make templates of patterns, see Cutting with Templates, *page 153.* Cut border strips lengthwise (parallel to the selvage). Because embroidery often distorts the foundation fabric, the border strips are cut larger than necessary. You'll trim them to the correct size after the embroidery is complete.

From gold print, cut:
- 4—2×42½" inner border strips
- 18—4¼" squares, cutting each diagonally twice in an X for 72 triangles total
- 9—3½" squares
- 4 of Pattern A

From beige print, cut:
- 4—5½×55" outer border strips
- 18—4¼" squares, cutting each diagonally twice in an X for 72 triangles total
- 36—3½" squares

From light beige print, cut:
- 2—14" squares, cutting each diagonally twice in an X for 8 setting triangles total
- 4—9½" setting squares

continued

- 2—7¼" squares, cutting each in half diagonally for 4 corner triangles total

From olive green print, cut:
- 1—25" square, cutting it into enough 2½"-wide bias strips to total 220" in length for binding (For details, see Cutting Bias Strips, *page 157*.)
- 1—18" square, cutting it into enough 1"-wide bias strips to total 220" in length for stem appliqués
- 76 of Pattern D
- 20 of Pattern E
- 8 of Pattern E reversed

From red moiré, cut:
- 4 of Pattern B
- 28 of Pattern F

From red print, cut:
- 4 of Pattern C

Assemble Ohio Star Blocks

1. Sew together two gold print triangles and two beige print triangles in pairs. Press seams toward gold print. Join pairs to make an hourglass unit (**Diagram 1**). The unit should be 3½" square including seam allowances. Repeat to make four hourglass units total.

Diagram 1

2. Referring to **Diagram 2**, lay out four hourglass units, four beige print 3½" squares, and one gold print 3½" square in three rows. Sew together pieces in each row. Press seams toward squares. Join rows to make an Ohio Star block. Press seams in one direction. The block should be 9½" square including seam allowances.

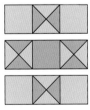

Diagram 2

3. Repeat steps 1 and 2 to make nine Ohio Star blocks total.

Assemble Quilt Center

1. Referring to **Diagram 3**, lay out nine Ohio Star blocks, four light beige print 9½" setting squares, and eight light beige print setting triangles in diagonal rows.

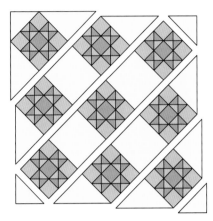

Diagram 3

2. Sew together pieces in each row. Press seams toward setting squares and triangles. Join rows. Press seams in one direction. Add four light beige print corner triangles to complete quilt center. Press seams toward corner triangles. The quilt center should be 38¾" square including seam allowances.

Appliqué Quilt Center

1. Prepare olive green print 1"-wide bias strips for appliqué by finger-pressing under ³⁄₁₆" seam allowances.

2. Cut prepared olive green strips into:
- 20—9"-long stem appliqués
- 4—6"-long stem appliqués
- 4—4"-long stem appliqués

3. Prepare gold print A flower centers, red moiré B flowers and F buds, red print C petals, and olive green print D, E, and E reversed leaf pieces by finger-pressing under ³⁄₁₆" seam allowances. You do not need to turn under edges that will be overlapped by other pieces.

4. Referring to **Appliqué Placement Diagram**, baste prepared appliqué pieces to quilt center.

5. Using matching threads and working from bottom layer to top, hand-appliqué pieces in place.

Add Embroidery

1. The Embroidery Verse Pattern is on *Pattern Sheet 2*. Enlarge Embroidery Verse Pattern to full size.

2. Center embroidery pattern for each side of quilt on a beige print 5½×55" outer border strip. Lightly trace using a red fine-point permanent marker.

3. Using two strands of red embroidery floss, stem-stitch lettering on each border strip.

To stem-stitch, pull needle up at A (**Stem Stitch Diagram**). Insert your needle back into fabric at B, about ⅜" away from A. Holding floss out of the way, bring your needle back up at C and pull floss through so it lies flat against the fabric. The distances between points A, B, and C should be equal. Pull with equal tautness after each stitch.

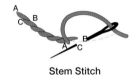

Stem Stitch

4. Centering the embroidery design, trim each embroidered outer border strip to measure 4½×52½" including seam allowances.

Add Borders

1. Aligning midpoints, sew together a gold print inner border strip and an embroidered outer border strip to make a border unit. Press seam toward gold strip.

2. Repeat Step 1 to make four border units total. Sew border units to quilt center, mitering corners to complete quilt top. (For details, see Mitered Border Corners, *page 156*.) Make sure that embroidered verse will be attached in correct order before sewing.

Finish Quilt

1. Layer quilt top, batting, and backing; baste. (For details, see Complete the Quilt, *page 159*.)

2. Quilt as desired. Petal shapes are stitched in the flower appliqués and a small meandering line is quilted around the stems and across the stars and background.

3. Bind with olive green print binding strips. (For details, see Complete the Quilt.)

Appliqué Placement Diagram

optional colors

Pastel Throw

When she saw this pattern, quilt tester Laura Boehnke knew exactly what fabrics she wanted to use: floral-theme pastels. Laura's first choice was a pale green print border fabric; then she selected the light print background. "For the Ohio Star blocks in the background, I used yellow plaids and prints," Laura says. She used a marbled light green for the stems.

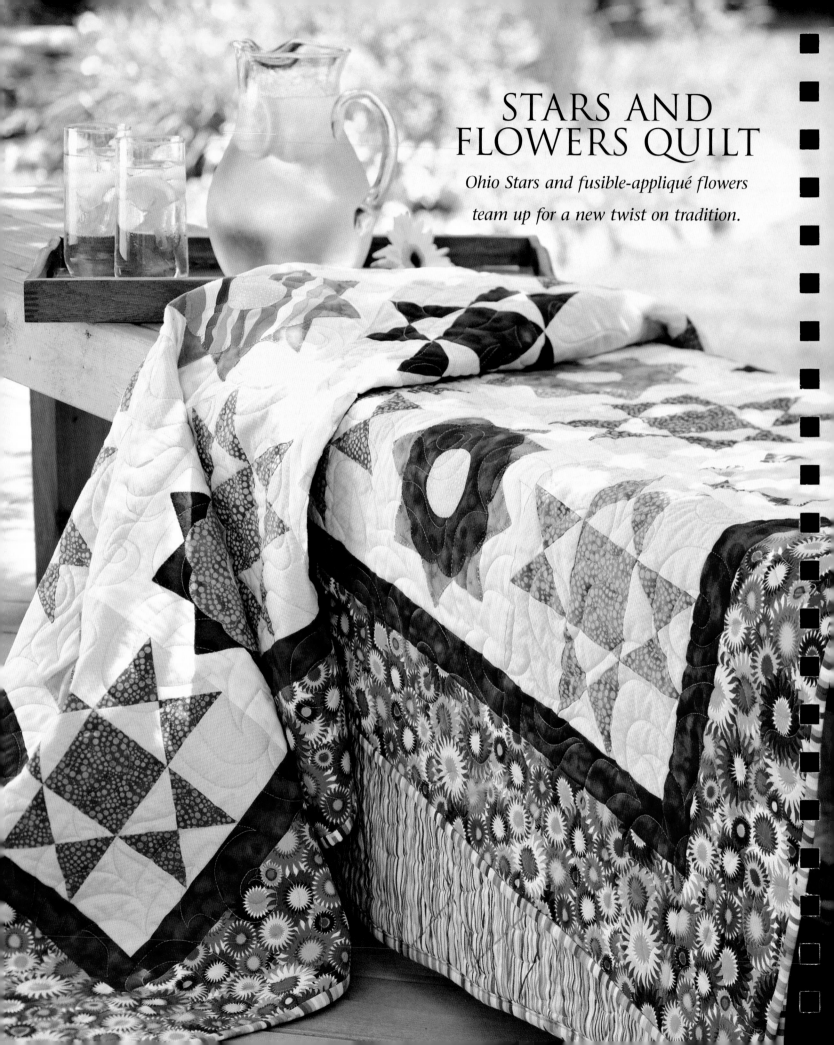

STARS AND FLOWERS QUILT

Ohio Stars and fusible-appliqué flowers

team up for a new twist on tradition.

Materials

4⅜ yards total assorted blue and green prints and

    stripes (star blocks, flower appliqués)

¼ yard yellow print (flower center appliqués)

2¼ yards beige print (star blocks)

2½ yards cream print (appliqué foundations)

⅝ yard mottled dark blue (inner border)

1⅝ yards blue print (outer border)

⅞ yard multicolor stripe (binding)

5⅝ yards backing fabric

83×101" batting

Fusible web

Finished quilt: 76½×94½"

Cut Fabrics

Cut pieces in the following order. This project uses "Ohio Memories" patterns on *Pattern Sheet 1*.

    To use fusible web for appliquéing, complete the following steps.

1. Lay fusible web, paper side up, over appliqué patterns. Use a pencil to trace patterns the number of times indicated in cutting instructions, leaving ½" between tracings. Cut out each fusible-web shape roughly ¼" outside traced lines.

2. Following manufacturer's instructions, press fusible-web shapes onto wrong sides of designated fabrics; let cool. Cut out fabric shapes on drawn lines. Peel off paper backings.

From assorted blue and green prints and stripes, cut:
• 64—4¼" squares, cutting each diagonally
    twice in an X for 256 triangles total
    (32 sets of 8 matching triangles)
• 32—3½" squares (one to match
    each set of triangles)
• 31 *each* of patterns B and C
From yellow print, cut:
• 31 of Pattern A
From beige print, cut:
• 64—4¼" squares, cutting each diagonally
    twice in an X for 256 triangles total
• 128—3½" squares

From cream print, cut:
• 31—9½" squares
From mottled dark blue, cut:
• 8—2×42" strips for inner border
From blue print, cut:
• 9—5½×42" strips for outer border
From multicolor stripe, cut:
• 9—2½×42" binding strips

Assemble Blocks

1. Referring to Assemble Ohio Star Blocks, *page 124*, steps 1 and 2, make 32 Ohio Star blocks using assorted blue and green print and stripe triangles and squares, and beige print triangles and squares. Match fabric in each block.

2. Referring to **Appliqué Placement Diagram**, arrange one each of pieces A, B, and C on each cream print 9½" square. Fuse all pieces in place.

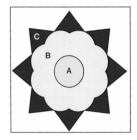

Appliqué Placement Diagram

3. Using matching thread, machine-appliqué block pieces in place for 31 appliqué blocks total.

Assemble Quilt Center

1. Referring to photo on *page 128*, lay out 32 Ohio Star blocks and 31 appliqué blocks in nine rows. Join pieces in each row. Press seams in one direction, alternating direction with each row.

2. Sew together rows to make quilt center. Press seams in one direction. The quilt center should be 63½×81½" including seam allowances.

Add Borders

1. Cut and piece mottled dark blue 2×42" strips to make:
• 2—2×81½" inner border strips
• 2—2×66½" inner border strips

2. Sew long inner border strips to long edges of quilt center. Add short inner border strips to remaining edges. Press all seams toward border.

continued

3. Cut and piece blue print 5½×42" strips to make:
- 2—5½×84½" outer border strips
- 2—5½×76½" outer border strips

4. Sew long outer border strips to long edges of quilt center. Add short outer border strips to remaining edges to complete quilt top. Press all seams toward outer border.

Finish Quilt

1. Layer quilt top, batting, and backing; baste. (For details, see Complete the Quilt, *page 159.*) Quilt as desired.

2. Bind with multicolor stripe binding strips. (For details, see Complete the Quilt.)

Ohio Memories

TEA TOWEL

Embellish a tea towel with a simple vine design.

Materials

Scraps of assorted green and pink prints
(leaf, flower, and vine appliqués)

Tea towel

¼ yard fusible web

Cut Fabrics

Cut pieces in the following order. This project uses "Ohio Memories" patterns and two additional patterns on *Pattern Sheet 1*. To achieve the same orientation, all patterns will need to be reversed for fusible web appliqué. To use fusible web for appliquéing, complete the following steps.

1. Lay fusible web, paper side up, over appliqué patterns. Use a pencil to trace patterns the number of times indicated in cutting instructions, leaving ½" between tracings. Cut out each fusible-web shape roughly ¼" outside traced lines.

2. Following manufacturer's instructions, press fusible-web shapes onto wrong sides of designated fabrics; let cool. Cut out fabric shapes on drawn lines. Peel off paper backings.

From green print, cut:
• 8 of Pattern D
• 4 of Pattern E
• 2 *each* of patterns G and H
From pink print, cut:
• 4 of Pattern F

Appliqué Tea Towel

Referring to **Appliqué Placement Diagram**, lay out appliqué pieces on each end of tea towel; fuse in place. Use matching thread to machine-satin-stitch around each appliqué shape.

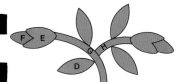

Appliqué Placement Diagram

SIGNS OF
Spring

Designer Tonee White put her spin on springtime with this fast and fun appliqué quilt. Tonee combined the appliquéing and quilting into one step to create this "appliquilt" wall hanging. Try your hand at this simple technique.

Materials

⅓ yard solid dark tan (appliqué, borders)

⅛ yard moss green plaid (borders)

½ yard muslin (appliqué foundation)

¼ yard tan plaid (appliqué foundation)

⅓ yard mottled light brown (appliqué foundation)

¼ yard dark tan plaid (appliqué foundation)

Scraps of assorted yellow-green, red, pink, blue, olive green, and gold prints (appliqués)

5½×12½" piece brown polka dot (basket appliqué)

18×22" piece (fat quarter) green print (appliqué)

⅓ yard dark brown print (binding)

1⅛ yards backing fabric

38×42" batting

Perle cotton No. 5: dark tan

Embroidery floss: dark green, red, gold, blue, and black

21 assorted buttons

Finished quilt: 31½×36"

Quantities are for 44/45"-wide, 100% cotton fabrics. Measurements include ¼" seam allowances. Sew with right sides together unless otherwise stated.

Designer Notes

Designer Tonee White's appliquilt technique involves layering a pieced quilt top with batting and backing, then appliquéing through all three layers. Using thread in a contrasting color gives the finished project a country look and disguises minor appliqué flaws, such as less-than-smooth curves. The instructions that follow incorporate Tonee's technique.

Cut Fabrics

Cut pieces in the following order. Patterns are on *Pattern Sheet 2*. To make pattern templates, see Cutting with Templates, *page 153.*

From solid dark tan, cut:
• 1—4½×36" rectangle
• 1—1¼×30" strip for stem appliqué
• 5—2¾" squares, cutting each diagonally twice in an X for 20 triangles total
• 13—1½×2½" rectangles

From moss green plaid, cut:
• 5—2¾" squares, cutting each diagonally twice in an X for 20 triangles total
• 14—1½×2½" rectangles

From muslin, cut:
• 1—15½×22½" rectangle

From tan plaid, cut:
• 1—6½×24" rectangle

From mottled light brown, cut:
• 1—21½×10½" rectangle

From dark tan plaid, cut:
• 1—6½×34" rectangle

continued

From assorted yellow-green prints, cut:
• 18 of Pattern O
• 1 *each* of patterns A and J

From assorted red and pink prints, cut:
• 1 *each* of patterns A, M, R, T, and U
• 2 *each* of patterns A reversed, B, H, I, and P
• 4 *each* of patterns E and Q
• 7 of Pattern Y

From assorted blue prints, cut:
• 1 *each* of patterns A and A reversed
• 2 *each* of patterns T and U
• 7 of Pattern Y

From assorted olive green prints, cut:
• 1—1¼×20" strip for stem appliqué
• 13 of Pattern O
• 4 *each* of patterns C, D, and D reversed
• 1 *each* of patterns A, G, and N

From assorted gold prints, cut:
• 1 *each* of patterns A reversed, F, J, K, and L

From brown polka dot, cut:
• 1 of Pattern S

From green print, cut:
• 1—10" square, cutting it into enough ¾"-wide bias strips to total 35" in length for stem appliqués (For details, see Cutting Bias Strips, *page 157*.)
• 3 of Pattern V
• 1 *each* of patterns W, W reversed, and X

From dark brown print, cut:
• 4—2½×42" binding strips

Assemble Borders

1. Referring to **Diagram 1**, sew together two solid dark tan triangles and two moss green plaid triangles in pairs. Press seams toward solid dark tan. Join pairs to make an hourglass unit. Press seam in one direction. The unit should be 2" square including seam allowances. Repeat to make 10 hourglass units total.

Diagram 1

2. Referring to **Quilt Assembly Diagram**, sew together 10 hourglass units in a row to make short border strip. The border should be 2×15½" including seam allowances.

3. Referring to **Quilt Assembly Diagram** and aligning long edges, sew together 13 solid dark tan 1½×2½" rectangles and 14 moss green plaid 1½×2½" rectangles, alternating colors, to make long border strip. Press seams toward solid dark tan. Trim border strip to measure 2½×27" including seam allowances.

Assemble Quilt Top

1. Referring to **Quilt Assembly Diagram**, sew short border strip to top edge of muslin 15½×22½" rectangle. Press seam toward muslin.

2. Sew tan plaid 6½×24" rectangle to right-hand edge of muslin rectangle to make quilt center. Press seam toward tan plaid rectangle.

3. Sew mottled light brown 21½×10½" rectangle to top edge of quilt center. Press seam toward mottled light brown.

4. Sew dark tan plaid 6½×34" rectangle to right-hand edge of quilt center. Press seam toward dark tan plaid.

Quilt Assembly Diagram

Signs of Spring

5. Sew long border strip to bottom edge of quilt center. Press seam toward quilt center.

6. Add solid dark tan 4½×36" rectangle to left-hand edge of quilt center to complete quilt top. Press seam toward solid dark tan.

Prepare and Bind Quilt Layers
1. Layer quilt top, batting, and backing; baste. (For details, see Complete the Quilt, *page 159*.)

2. Quilt as desired. Tonee machine-quilted in the ditch between all pieces using monofilament or matching thread. Then she used dark tan perle cotton to hand-quilt a 2"-wide diagonal grid in the mottled light brown 21½×10½" rectangle, circles of various sizes in the solid dark tan 4½×36" rectangle, and 1"-wide parallel lines in the tan plaid 6½×24" rectangle and dark tan plaid 6½×34" rectangle. She also hand-quilted a 3×5½" block grid in the muslin rectangle.

3. Bind with dark brown print binding strips. (For details, see Complete the Quilt.)

Make Yo-Yo Flowers
1. Thread a needle with a color that matches a Y circle; tie a heavy knot at the end. Use your fingers to fold under about ¼" of the circle for a hem. Take running stitches (approximately four stitches per inch) all the way around edge of circle; do not cut your thread (**Diagram 2**). Stitch just inside fold line so fabric will gather nicely.

2. Pull thread, gathering edge to center with wrong side of fabric inside (**Diagram 3**), to make a yo-yo. Pull thread tight and knot it. Work fabric and gathers to make yo-yo lie flat. Press yo-yo lightly.

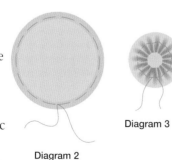

Diagram 3

Diagram 2

3. Repeat steps 1 and 2 with remaining Y fabric circles to make 14 yo-yos total.

Appliquilt Motifs
1. Cut green print bias strips into five stems. Referring to photo on *page 130* and **Quilt Assembly Diagram**, pin appliqué pieces and stems in place on pieced quilt top.

2. To appliqué all pieces except for yo-yos and E circles, knot end of an 18" length of dark tan perle cotton. Starting with your needle underneath an appliqué piece and ¼" inside appliqué line, bring your needle to top, hiding knot below appliqué piece. Stitching through all layers and turning under edges of appliqué piece with your needle as you work, straight-stitch appliqué piece to quilt top. You'll be appliquéing and quilting in one step. Your stitches, perpendicular to folded-under edge, should be ⅛" to ¼" apart. Stitches will resemble blanket stitching, although thread won't run parallel to appliqué.

3. Using matching thread, tack yo-yos in place.

4. To make "puffy" flowers, transfer dashed line on Pattern E onto quilt top where you want your puffy flowers to be.

5. Pin center of a fabric E circle to center of a smaller drawn circle. Appliqué fabric E circle to quilt top on dashed line, gathering slightly as you go.

6. Using a contrasting color of floss and a square knot, tack fabric in a few places on top of puffy flowers. Clip threads, leaving short tails.

7. Repeat steps 5 and 6 for each puffy flower.

Embroider and Finish Quilt
1. Using three strands of dark green embroidery floss, add straight stitches around bases of mushrooms for grass.

2. Referring to photo on *page 130* and using three strands of contrasting embroidery floss, add stitching details to hearts and pears.

3. Tonee used a series of backstitches, lazy daisy stitches, and French knots to create flowers in appliquéd flower pots.
   To make a lazy daisy stitch (**Lazy Daisy Diagram**), pull needle up at A, leaving a loop of floss on fabric surface. Insert needle back into fabric at B, about 1⁄16" away from A. Bring needle tip out at C and loop trailing floss under

Lazy Daisy

continued

needle tip, keeping floss as flat as possible. Gently pull needle and trailing floss until loop lies flat against fabric. Push needle through to back at D.

French Knot

To make a French knot (**French Knot Diagram**), pull floss through at A, the point where a knot is desired. Wrap floss around needle two or three times without twisting it. (The more floss wrapped around the needle, the bigger the resulting French knot.) Insert tip of needle into fabric at B, ¹⁄₁₆" away from A. Gently push floss wraps down needle to meet fabric. Pull needle and trailing floss through fabric slowly and smoothly.

4. Sew 21 assorted buttons to quilt top where desired to finish quilt.

WOOL PILLOW

Brightly colored wool and homespun linen add to the charm of this folk art pillow.

Materials

⅝ yard tan heavy homespun (appliqué foundation, pillow back)

5½×12½" piece brown felted wool (basket appliqué)

3×26" piece green plaid felted wool (stem appliqués)

Scraps of assorted felted wool in dark green, pink, purple, red, blue, yellow, and orange (appliqués)

130 black seed beads

3 buttons

Embroidery floss: brown, green, gold, purple, blue, and red

12×20" pillow form

Freezer paper

Finished pillow: 12×20"

Cut Fabrics

Cut pieces in the following order. This project uses "Signs of Spring" patterns plus an additional pattern on *Pattern Sheet 2*.

To felt wool, machine-wash it in a hot-water-wash, cold-rinse cycle with a small amount of detergent; machine-dry on high heat; steam-press.

To use freezer-paper templates for cutting appliqué pieces, complete the following steps.

1. Lay freezer paper, shiny side down, over patterns. Use a pencil to trace each pattern the number of times indicated in cutting instructions, leaving ½" between tracings. Cut out freezer-paper shapes roughly ¼" outside drawn lines.

2. Using a hot, dry iron, press each freezer-paper shape, shiny side down, onto right side of designated fabric; let cool. Cut out fabric shapes on drawn lines. Peel off freezer paper.

From tan heavy homespun, cut:
• 1—13×21" rectangle
• 2—13" squares
From brown wool, cut:
• 1 of Pattern S
From green plaid wool, cut:
• 5—⅜×16" strips for stem appliqués
• 3 of Pattern V

From dark green wool, cut:
• 1 *each* of patterns W, W reversed, and X
From assorted wools in pink, purple, red, blue, yellow, and orange, cut:
• 3 *each* of patterns T and U
• 14 of Pattern Z

Appliqué Pillow Top

1. Referring to **Appliqué Placement Diagram**, arrange appliqué shapes on tan heavy homespun 13×21" appliqué foundation, trimming green plaid ⅜×16" strips to desired lengths. Baste or pin in place.

Appliqué Placement Diagram

2. Using one strand of matching floss and working from bottom to top, whipstitch appliqués in place, except for Z flowers.

3. Using one strand of green floss and a running stitch, secure black seed beads through centers of leaves to make lines.

4. Stitch four or five black seed beads to center of each Z flower to secure in place.

5. Stitch buttons to right-hand side of basket to complete pillow top. Press appliqués gently from back side of pillow top.

Finish Pillow

1. Press under ½" along one 13" edge of tan heavy homespun 13" squares. Press under an additional ½" and stitch in place to hem pillow back pieces.

2. Overlap hemmed edges by about 3"; pin pillow back to pillow top, aligning raw edges. Using ½" seam allowance, sew pieces together along all four edges to make pillow cover.

3. Turn right side out. Gently press. Insert pillow form.

SPRINGTIME BANNER

Combine just a few simple elements from the "Signs of Spring" quilt

to make a cheerful welcome for your home.

Materials

⅓ yard cream print (appliqué foundation,

    hourglass units, border)

⅓ yard gold print (appliqué foundation,

    hourglass units, border)

Scraps of assorted green, purple, red, and pink

    prints and plaids (appliqués)

18×22" piece (fat quarter) dark green plaid

    (binding)

½ yard backing fabric

18×42" batting

2 buttons

Fusible web

Finished quilt: 12½×36½"

Cut Fabrics

Cut pieces in the following order. This project uses "Signs of Spring" patterns on *Pattern Sheet 2.*

    To use fusible web for appliquéing, complete the following steps.

1. Lay fusible web, paper side up, over patterns. Use a pencil to trace each pattern the number of times indicated in cutting instructions, leaving ½" between tracings. Cut out each fusible-web shape roughly ¼" outside traced lines.

2. Following manufacturer's instructions, press fusible-web shapes onto wrong sides of designated fabrics; let cool. Cut out fabric shapes on drawn lines. Peel off paper backings.

From cream print, cut:
- 1—6½×34½" rectangle
- 12—2¾" squares, cutting each diagonally twice in an X for 48 triangles total
- 6—1½×2½" rectangles

From gold print, cut:
- 1—6½×25½" rectangle
- 12—2¾" squares, cutting each diagonally twice in an X for 48 triangles total
- 6—1½×2½" rectangles

From assorted green prints and plaids, cut:
- 1—2×30" strip for stem appliqué
- 1—2×20" strip for stem appliqué
- 31 of Pattern O

From assorted purple, red, and pink prints and plaids, cut:
- 2 of Pattern P
- 4 of Pattern Q
- 1 of Pattern R

From dark green plaid, cut:
- Enough 2½"-wide bias strips to total 110" for binding (For details, see Cutting Bias Strips, *page 157.*)

Assemble Quilt Top

1. Referring to Assemble Borders, *page 132,* Step 1, and using cream print triangles and gold print triangles, make 24 hourglass units total.

2. Referring to photo *opposite* for placement, lay out hourglass units in six rows. Sew together pieces in each row. Press seams in one direction, alternating direction with each row. Join rows to make hourglass section. Press seams in one direction. The hourglass section should be 6½×9½" including seam allowances.

3. Aligning short edges, sew hourglass section to top edge of gold print 6½×25½" rectangle. Press seam toward gold print.

4. Add cream print 6½×34½" rectangle to right-hand edge of Step 3 unit. Press seam toward cream print rectangle.

5. Alternating colors, sew together six cream print 1½×2½" rectangles and six gold print 1½×2½" rectangles to make a border strip. Press seams toward gold print.

6. Sew border strip to bottom edge of pieced Step 4 unit to complete quilt top. Press seam away from border.

Appliqué Quilt Top

1. Fold green plaid 2×20" strip in half lengthwise with wrong side inside; press. Stitch ¼" from long raw edge **(Diagram 4)**. Trim seam allowance to ⅛". Refold strip, centering seam in back. Press flat to make short stem appliqué. Repeat with green print 2×30" strip to make long stem appliqué.

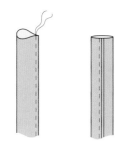

Diagram 4

2. Referring to photo *right*, arrange appliqué pieces on quilt top. Fuse in place.

3. Using matching thread and working from bottom layer to top, machine-blanket-stitch around appliqués.

Finish Quilt

1. Layer quilt top, batting, and backing; baste. (For details, see Complete the Quilt, *page 159*.)

2. Quilt as desired. This project is machine-quilted in the ditch around all appliqués. Hand-sew buttons to flower centers.

3. Bind with dark green plaid binding strips. (For details, see Complete the Quilt.)

PATCHWORK
Primer

Large floral appliqués are a pleasing contrast to the bold

Nine-Patch pattern in this original design by Ohio quiltmaker Kim Diehl.

Materials

2 yards total assorted dark prints (blocks)

7¾ yards wheat print (blocks, borders, binding)

⅝ yard green print (vine appliqués)

2⅛ yards total assorted cranberry prints
   (flower appliqués)

⅝ yard wheat-and-cranberry print
   (flower appliqués)

⅜ yard blue print (flower center appliqués)

18×22" piece (fat quarter) gold print (flower
   center appliqués)

½ yard light green print (flower center appliqués,
   leaf appliqués)

7⅞ yards backing fabric

94×106" batting

Freezer paper

Fabric glue stick

Water-erasable marker

Perle cotton No. 8: wheat

Finished quilt: 87½×99½"
Finished block: 6" square

Quantities are for 44/45"-wide, 100% cotton fabrics. Measurements include ¼" seam allowances. Sew with right sides together unless otherwise stated.

Designer Notes

Nine-Patch blocks serve as the primary design element in this scrappy quilt. Simple cornerstone setting blocks create the overall lattice pattern, and red flowers dress it up. "I love the Nine-Patch block," designer Kim Diehl says. "I find it a versatile block. Depending on color choices or the way you set it into your quilt, it can give you a number of different looks."

Kim used look-alike reds for the flowers. "I wanted to keep that scrappy feel, yet I was afraid it could become too busy," she says. "So I stayed in the red range."

This design lends itself easily to many different color schemes. "You could use a more planned scrappy look, where the Nine-Patch blocks are scrappy and the setting blocks are all the same," Kim says. "Or you could do it with two colors for a very geometric, graphically strong look."

continued

Cut Fabrics

Cut pieces in the following order. Cut border strips lengthwise (parallel to the selvage).

From assorted dark prints, cut:
- 49—2½" squares
- 50 sets of one 3½" square and four 2" squares for blocks
- 22 sets of one 3½" square and two 2" squares for pieced borders

From wheat print, cut:
- 2—12½×87½" strips for outer border
- 2—12½×75½" strips for outer border
- 10—2½×42" binding strips
- 22—3½×9½" rectangles
- 98—2½×6½" rectangles
- 22—2×6½" rectangles
- 218—2×3½" rectangles
- 98—2½" squares

Assemble Nine-Patch Blocks

I. Referring to **Diagram 1**, lay out one set of dark print squares (one 3½" and four 2" squares) and four wheat print 2×3½" rectangles in rows.

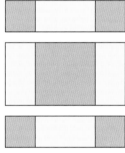

Diagram 1

2. Sew together pieces in each row. Press seams toward dark print squares. Join rows to make a Nine-Patch block. Press seams in one direction. The Nine-Patch block should be 6½" square including seam allowances.

3. Repeat steps 1 and 2 to make 50 Nine-Patch blocks total.

Assemble Setting Blocks

I. Referring to **Diagram 2**, lay out one dark print 2½" square, two wheat print 2½" squares, and two wheat print 2½×6½" rectangles.

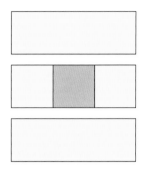

Diagram 2

2. Sew together squares in middle row. Press seams toward darker square. Sew rectangles to middle row to make a setting block. Press seams toward rectangles. The setting block should be 6½" square including seam allowances.

3. Repeat steps 1 and 2 to make 49 setting blocks total.

Assemble Quilt Center

I. Referring to photo *opposite*, lay out Nine-Patch blocks and setting blocks in 11 horizontal rows, alternating blocks in each row.

2. Sew together blocks in each row. Press seams toward Nine-Patch blocks. Join rows to complete quilt center. Press seams toward rows that begin and end with Nine-Patch blocks. The quilt center should be 54½×66½" including seam allowances.

Assemble and Add Pieced Borders

The inner and middle borders are designed to form partial Nine-Patch blocks to which the appliqué vines in the outer border are anchored.

I. Referring to photo *opposite*, sew together six wheat print 2×6½" rectangles, five wheat print 2×3½" rectangles, and five pairs of dark print 2" squares to make a long inner border. Press seams toward dark print squares. Repeat to make a second long inner border.

2. Join long inner borders to long edges of quilt center. Press seams toward inner border.

3. Referring again to photo, sew together five wheat print 2×6½" rectangles, four wheat print 2×3½" rectangles, four pairs of dark print 2" squares, and two additional dark print 2" squares to make a short inner border (you'll have two 2" squares left over). Press seams toward dark print squares. Repeat to make a second short inner border.

4. Sew short inner borders to remaining edges of quilt center. Press seams toward inner border.

5. Sew together six wheat print 3½×9½" rectangles and five dark print 3½" squares to make a long middle border. (See photo on *page 141;* match dark print squares with inner border dark print squares.) Press seams toward dark print squares. Repeat to make a second long middle border.

6. Join long middle borders to long edges of quilt center. Press seams toward middle border.

7. Sew together five wheat print 3½×9½" rectangles and six dark print 3½" squares to make a short middle border. (See photo; match dark print squares with inner border dark print squares.) Press seams toward dark print squares. Repeat to make a second short middle border.

8. Sew short middle borders to remaining edges of quilt center. Press seams toward middle border. The quilt center should be 63½×75½" including seam allowances.

Cut and Prepare Appliqués

The appliqué patterns are on *Pattern Sheet 1.* Kim used a freezer-paper method to prepare appliqué pieces. The instructions that follow are for this method.

   The number of pieces indicated for Pattern F is approximate, as the leaves are placed randomly along the vines. Use more or less, to your liking.

I. Lay freezer paper, shiny side down, over patterns. Trace each pattern the number of times indicated in cutting instructions. Cut out freezer-paper shapes on drawn lines.

2. Place a small amount of fabric glue on dull side of freezer-paper templates and position on wrong sides of designated fabrics, leaving ½" between shapes. Cut out each fabric shape about ¼" beyond freezer-paper edges.

3. Use point of a hot, dry iron to fold seam allowances under and press them onto shiny side of freezer-paper templates. Clip curves as necessary.

From green print, cut:
• 52—1½×9" strips
From assorted cranberry prints, cut:
• 104 of Pattern A
From wheat-and-cranberry print, cut:
• 104 of Pattern B
From blue print, cut:
• 26 of Pattern C
From gold print, cut:
• 26 of Pattern D
From light green print, cut:
• 26 of Pattern E
• 90 of Pattern F

4. Fold green print strips in half lengthwise, wrong sides together; press. Stitch ¼" from raw edges (**Diagram 3**). Trim seam allowances to ⅛". Refold strips to center stitched seams, forming vine appliqués; press.

Diagram 3

Appliqué and Add Outer Border

Kim appliquéd the outer border strips prior to joining them to the quilt center.

I. Fold each wheat print outer border strip in half lengthwise and lightly press a crease in the fabric.

2. Lay out short outer border strips along long edges of quilt center. Lay out long outer border strips along remaining edges. With a water-erasable marker, mark a small line in the seam allowance of each outer border strip at the center of each dark print 3½" square in the middle border.

3. Match up each pair of adjacent marked lines and press a vertical crease in the fabric. (Creased lines will be placement guides for laying out appliqué pieces; see gray lines on **Border Placement Diagram.**) On long outer border strips only, make an additional vertical crease 6¼" from each end.

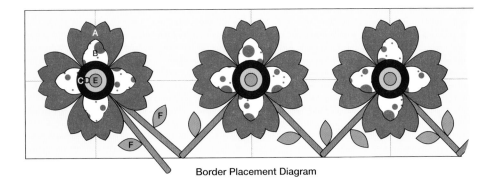

Border Placement Diagram

4. Place an E flower center appliqué over each intersection of creased lines on outer border strips. Referring to **Border Placement Diagram**, position two vine appliqués in each space between flower centers, beginning at mark in seam allowance and angling up to flower centers. Remove flower center appliqués, then affix vines to border strips using a fabric glue stick.

5. Hand- or machine-appliqué vines in place. Leave the vine appliqué at each end of long outer border strips partially unstitched until border strips are joined to the quilt center.

6. At each intersection of creased lines, arrange four A flower appliqués, four B flower appliqués, and one *each* of C, D, and E flower center appliqués **(Border Placement Diagram)**. Arrange F leaf appliqués as desired. Pin or baste all pieces in place.

7. Working from bottom layer to top, use matching thread to hand- or machine-stitch each appliqué shape in place, leaving an opening to remove each template as you go (for details, see Step 8). Also leave openings between Pattern A pieces on end of each short border strip to allow remaining vines to be added after border strips are joined to quilt center.

8. Remove freezer-paper templates as follows:
- For hand appliqué, leave a ½" opening along edge of shape. Using your needle, gently loosen freezer paper from fabric and pull it through opening. Hand-stitch opening closed.
- For machine appliqué, trim away border strip from behind, leaving a ¼" seam allowance. With your fingertip or end of your needle, loosen freezer paper from fabric and gently peel it away.

9. Join short appliquéd border strips to long edges of quilt center. Then add long appliquéd border strips to remaining edges to complete quilt top. Leave two small openings to accommodate appliqué vines that are added in Step 8. Press all seam allowances toward quilt center.

10. Add remaining vines and stitch down any appliqués that were left loose to accommodate seams.

11. Lightly spray appliquéd border with water if necessary to remove any visible marked lines.

Finish Quilt
1. Layer quilt top, batting, and backing; baste. (For details, see Complete the Quilt, *page 159.*)

2. Quilt as desired. Kathy Ockerman of Idaho Falls, Idaho, machine-quilted the quilt center with a small stipple interspersed with randomly placed feathered plumes; she added a small stipple in the outer borders. Kim asked her to leave specific areas unquilted.

"I leave appliqués or darker print areas in my blocks for hand quilting," she says. "At a glance, the quilt has the appearance of being hand-quilted." Kim hand-quilted around the flower centers using a No. 5 embroidery needle and big stitches in wheat perle cotton No. 8 to emphasize the appliqué shapes.

3. Bind with wheat print binding strips. (For details, see Complete the Quilt.)

Patchwork Primer

continued

optional sizes

If you'd like to make this quilt in a size other than for a full/queen bed, use the information *below*.

Alternate quilt sizes	Large Wall	Twin
Number of Nine-Patch blocks	25	32
Number of blocks wide by long	7×7	7×9
Number of setting blocks	24	31
Number of border appliqués	20	22
Finished size	75½" square	75½×87½"

Yardage Requirements

Total of assorted dark prints	1¼ yards	1⅜ yards
Wheat print	6 yards	6⅔ yards
Green print	⅝ yard	⅝ yard
Total of assorted cranberry prints	1¾ yards	1⅞ yards
Wheat-and-cranberry print	½ yard	⅝ yard
Blue print	⅓ yard	⅓ yard
Gold print	1 fat quarter	1 fat quarter
Light green print	⅓ yard	⅓ yard
Backing fabric	4⅝ yards	5¼ yards
Batting	82" square	82×94"

optional colors

Beautiful Blues

For her version of "Patchwork Primer," quilt tester Laura Boehnke controlled the scrappy look by using prints with a range of colors in the larger squares, while the smaller squares are basically one color.

"On a quilt with more blocks, the chain effect of the colors would stand out more," she says of this color scheme.

TABLE TOPPER

Fresh spring flowers blossom before your eyes on this machine-appliquéd accent piece.

Materials

¾ yard solid cream (appliqué foundations)

½ yard blue print (flower appliqués)

Scraps of assorted yellow, blue, and green prints

    (flower, vine, and leaf appliqués)

1⅛ yards blue floral border stripe (border)

⅓ yard blue mini-print (binding)

1¼ yards backing fabric

42" square batting

¾ yard fusible web

Finished quilt: 35½" square

Cut Fabrics

Cut pieces in the following order. This project uses "Patchwork Primer" patterns on *Pattern Sheet 1*. Cut border strips lengthwise (parallel to the selvage).

To use fusible web for appliquéing, complete the following steps.

1. Lay fusible web, paper side up, over appliqué patterns. Use a pencil to trace patterns the number of times indicated in cutting instructions, leaving ½" between tracings. Cut out each fusible-web shape roughly ¼" outside traced lines.

2. Following manufacturer's instructions, press fusible-web shapes onto wrong sides of designated fabrics; let cool. Cut out fabric shapes on drawn lines. Peel off paper backings.

From solid cream, cut:
• 4—12½" squares
From blue print, cut:
• 16 of Pattern A
From assorted yellow prints, cut:
• 16 of Pattern B
• 4 of Pattern C
From assorted blue prints, cut:
• 4 of Pattern D

From assorted green prints, cut:
• 8 of Pattern F
• 4 of Pattern E
• 4—1½×9" strips
From blue floral border stripe, cut:
• 4—6×40" strips for border
From blue mini-print, cut:
• 4—2½×42" binding strips

Appliqué and Assemble Quilt Center

1. Referring to Cut and Prepare Appliqués on *page 142*, Step 4, use assorted green print 1½×9" strips to make four vine appliqués.

2. Referring to **Appliqué Placement Diagram**, pin vine appliqués in place and layer remaining appliqué pieces on each solid cream 12½" square. Fuse in place. Using matching thread, machine-appliqué pieces in place.

Appliqué Placement Diagram

3. Referring to photo *opposite*, sew appliqué blocks together in pairs. Press seams in opposite directions. Join pairs to complete quilt center. Press seam in one direction.

Add Border

With midpoints aligned, sew two blue floral border stripe 6×40" border strips to opposite edges of quilt center, beginning and ending seams ¼" from corners. Add remaining blue floral border stripe 6×40" border strips to remaining edges, mitering corners to complete the quilt top. (For details, see Mitered Border Corners, *page 156*.) Press seams toward border.

Finish Quilt

1. Layer quilt top, batting, and backing; baste. (For details, see Complete the Quilt, *page 159*.)

2. Quilt as desired. Machine-quilter Kelly Edwards echo-quilted around the flowers in the quilt center and outline-stitched the large floral print in the border.

3. Bind with blue mini-print binding strips. (For details, see Complete the Quilt.)

SQUARED-UP BED QUILT

Bold colors set against a black background give this simple quilt a dramatic look.

Materials

6⅓ yards mottled black (blocks, sashing, border, binding)

⅞ yard total assorted blue, purple, red, orange, and green prints (blocks)

7⅓ yards backing fabric

88×94" batting

Finished quilt: 81½×87½"

Cut Fabrics

Cut pieces in the following order. Cut borders, sashing and binding lengthwise (parallel to the selvage).

From mottled black, cut:
• 4—2½×87" binding strips
• 2—6½×81½" border strips
• 2—6½×75½" border strips
• 12—3½×69½" sashing strips
• 65—3½×9½" rectangles
• 13—3½×6½" rectangles
From assorted blue, purple, red, orange, and green prints, cut:
• 78—3½" squares

continued

Assemble Quilt Center

I. Sew together five mottled black 3½×9½" rectangles, one mottled black 3½×6½" rectangle, and six assorted blue, purple, red, orange, and green print 3½" squares in a row (**Diagram 4**). Press seams toward mottled black rectangles. Repeat to make 13 pieced rows total.

Diagram 4

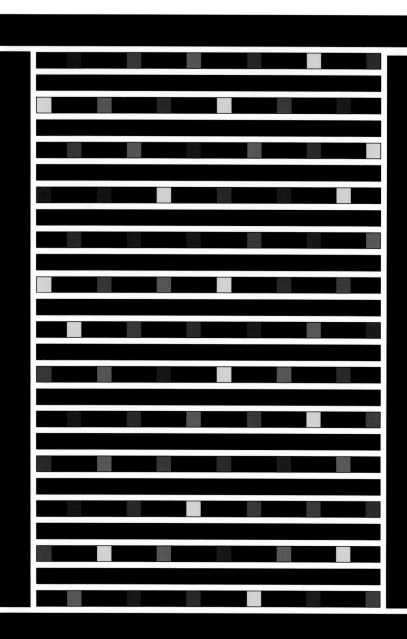

Quilt Assembly Diagram

2. Referring to **Quilt Assembly Diagram**, lay out 13 pieced rows and 12 mottled black 3½×69½" sashing strips, alternating rows and sashing strips and reversing placement of pieced rows as shown. Join to make quilt center. Press seams toward sashing. Quilt center should be 69½×75½" including seam allowances.

Add Border

I. Sew mottled black 6½×75½" border strips to long edges of quilt center.

2. Sew mottled black 6½×81½" border strips to remaining edges to complete quilt top. Press all seams toward border.

Finish Quilt

I. Layer quilt top, batting, and backing; baste. (For details, see Complete the Quilt, *page 159.*) Quilt as desired.

2. Bind with mottled black binding strips. (For details, see Complete the Quilt.)

QUILTER'S SCHOOLHOUSE

GETTING STARTED

Before you begin any project, collect the tools and materials you'll need in one place.

Basic Tools
1. Rotary-cutting mat
2. Template plastic
3. Template
4. Acrylic rulers
5. Chalk marker
6. Marking pencil
7. Water-erasable marker
8. Rotary cutter
9. Bias bars
10. Quilting stencils

Tools

CUTTING

Acrylic ruler: To aid in making perfectly straight cuts with a rotary cutter, choose a ruler of thick, clear plastic. Many sizes are available. A 6×24" ruler marked in ¼" increments with 30°, 45°, and 60° angles is a good first purchase.

Rotary-cutting mat: A rotary cutter should always be used with a mat designed specifically for it. The mat protects the table and helps keep the fabric from shifting while you cut. Often these mats are described as self-healing, meaning the blade does not leave slash marks or grooves in the surface, even after repeated usage. While many sizes and shapes are available, a 16×23" mat marked with a 1" grid, with hash marks at ⅛" increments and 45° and 60° angles, is a good choice.

Rotary cutter: The round blade of a rotary cutter will cut up to six fabric layers at once. Because the blade is so sharp, be sure to purchase one with a safety guard and keep the guard over the blade when you're not cutting. The blade can be removed from the handle and replaced when it gets dull. Commonly available in three sizes, a good first blade is a 45 mm.

Scissors: You'll need one pair for cutting fabric and another for cutting paper and plastic.

Pencils and other marking tools: Marks made with special quilt markers are easy to remove after sewing.

Template plastic: This slightly frosted plastic comes in sheets about ¹⁄₁₆" thick.

PIECING

Iron and ironing board

Sewing thread: Use 100% cotton thread.

Sewing machine: Any machine in good working order with well-adjusted tension will produce pucker-free patchwork seams.

APPLIQUÉ

Fusible web: Instead of the traditional method, secure cutout shapes to the background of an appliqué block with this iron-on adhesive.

Hand-sewing needles: For hand appliqué, most quilters like fine quilting needles.

HAND QUILTING

Frame or hoop: You'll get smaller, more even stitches if you stretch your quilt as you stitch. A frame supports the quilt's weight, ensures even tension, and frees both your hands for stitching. However, once set up, it cannot be disassembled until the quilting is complete. Quilting hoops are more portable and less expensive.

Quilting needles: A "between" or quilting needle is short with a small eye. Common sizes are 8, 9, and 10; size 8 is best for beginners.

Quilting thread: Quilting thread is stronger than sewing thread.

Thimble: This finger cover relieves the pressure required to push a needle through several layers of fabric and batting.

MACHINE QUILTING

Darning foot: You may find this tool, also called a hopper foot, in your sewing machine's accessory kit. If not, have your machine model and brand available when you go to purchase one. It is used for free-motion stitching.

Safety pins: They hold the layers together during quilting.

Table: Use a large work surface that's level with your machine bed.

Thread: Use 100% cotton quilting thread, cotton-wrapped polyester quilting thread, or fine nylon monofilament thread.

Walking foot: This sewing-machine accessory helps you keep long, straight quilting lines smooth and pucker-free.

Choose Your Fabrics

It is no surprise that most quilters prefer 100% cotton fabrics for quiltmaking. Cotton fabric minimizes seam distortion, presses crisply, and is easy to quilt. Most patterns, including those in this book, specify quantities for 44/45"-wide fabrics unless otherwise noted. Our projects call for a little extra yardage in length to allow for minor errors and slight shrinkage.

Prepare Your Fabrics

There are conflicting opinions about the need to prewash fabric. The debate is a modern one because most antique quilts were made with unwashed fabric. However, the dyes and sizing used today are unlike those used a century ago.

Prewashing fabric offers quilters certainty as its main advantage. Today's fabrics resist bleeding and shrinkage, but some of both can occur in some fabrics. Some quilters find prewashed fabric easier to quilt. If you choose to prewash your fabric, press it well before cutting.

Other quilters prefer the crispness of unwashed fabric, especially for machine piecing. And, if you use fabrics with the same fiber content throughout a quilt, then any shrinkage that occurs in its first washing should be uniform. Some quilters find this small amount of shrinkage desirable, since it gives a quilt a slightly puckered, antique look.

We recommend prewashing a scrap of each fabric to test it for shrinkage and bleeding. If you choose to prewash an entire fabric piece, unfold it to a single layer. Wash it in warm water, which will allow the fabric to shrink and/or bleed. If the fabric bleeds, rinse it until the water runs clear. Do not use it in a quilt if it hasn't stopped bleeding. Hang the fabric to dry, or tumble it in the dryer until slightly damp; press well.

Select the Batting

For a small beginner project, a thin cotton batting is a good choice. It has a tendency to "stick" to fabric, so it requires less basting. Also, it's easy to stitch. It's wise to follow the stitch density (maximum distance between rows of stitching required to keep the batting from shifting and wadding up inside the quilt) recommendation printed on the packaging.

Polyester batting is lightweight and readily available. In general, it springs back to its original height when compressed, adding a puffiness to quilts. It tends to "beard" (work out between the weave of the fabric) more than natural fibers. Polyester fleece is denser and works well for pillow tops and place mats.

Wool batting has good loft retention and absorbs moisture, making it ideal for cool, damp climates. Read the label carefully before purchasing a wool batting; it may require special handling.

ROTARY CUTTING

We've taken the guesswork out of rotary cutting with this primer.

Plan for Cutting

Quilt-Lovers' Favorites® instructions list pieces in the order in which they should be cut to make the best use of your fabrics. Always consider the fabric grain before cutting. The arrow on a pattern piece or template indicates which direction the fabric grain should run. One or more straight sides of the pattern piece or template should follow the fabric's lengthwise or crosswise grain.

The lengthwise grain, parallel to the selvage (the tightly finished edge), has the least amount of stretch. (Do not use the selvage of a woven fabric in a quilt. When washed, it may shrink more than the rest of the fabric.) Crosswise grain, perpendicular to the selvage, has a little more give. The edge of any pattern piece that will be on the outside of a block or quilt should always be cut on the lengthwise grain. Be sure to press the fabric before cutting to remove any wrinkles or folds.

Using a Rotary Cutter

When cutting, keep an even pressure on the rotary cutter and make sure the blade is touching the edge of the ruler. The less you *continued* move your fabric when cutting, the more accurate you'll be.

SQUARING UP THE FABRIC EDGE

Before rotary-cutting fabric into strips, it is imperative that one fabric edge be made straight, or squared up. Since all subsequent cuts will be measured from this straight edge, squaring up the fabric edge is an important step. There are several techniques for squaring up an edge, some of which involve the use of a pair of rulers. For clarity and simplicity, we have chosen to describe a single-ruler technique here. *Note:* The instructions are for right-handers.

1. Lay your fabric on the rotary mat with the right side down and one selvage edge away from you. Fold the fabric with the wrong side inside and the selvages together. Fold the fabric in half again, lining up the fold with the selvage edges. Lightly hand-crease all of the folds.

2. Position the folded fabric on the cutting mat with the selvage edges away from you and the bulk of the fabric length to your left. With the ruler on top of the fabric, align a horizontal grid line on the ruler with the lower folded fabric edge, leaving about 1" of fabric exposed along the ruler's right-hand edge (see **Photo 1**). Do not worry about or try to align the uneven raw edges along the right-hand side of the fabric. *Note:* If the grid lines on the cutting mat interfere with your ability to focus on the ruler grid lines, turn your cutting mat over and work on the unmarked side.

3. Hold the ruler firmly in place with your left hand, keeping your fingers away from the right-hand edge and spreading your fingers apart slightly. Apply pressure to the ruler with your fingertips to prevent it from slipping as you cut. With the ruler firmly in place, hold the rotary cutter so the blade is touching the right-hand edge of the ruler. Roll the blade along the ruler edge, beginning just off the folded edge and pushing the cutter away from you, toward the selvage edge.

4. The fabric strip to the right of the ruler's edge should be cut cleanly away, leaving you with a straight edge from which you can measure all subsequent cuts. Do not pick up the fabric once the edge is squared; instead, turn the cutting mat to rotate the fabric and begin cutting strips.

CUTTING AND SUBCUTTING STRIPS

To use a rotary cutter to its greatest advantage, first cut a strip of fabric, then subcut the strip into specific sizes. For example, if your instructions say to cut forty 2" squares, follow these steps.

1. First cut a 2"-wide strip crosswise on the fabric. Assuming you have squared up the fabric edge as described earlier, you can turn your cutting mat clockwise 180° with the newly squared-up edge on your left and the excess fabric on the right. Place the ruler on top of the fabric.

2. Align the 2" grid mark on the ruler with the squared-up edge of the fabric (see **Photo 2**). *Note:* Align only the vertical grid mark and the fabric raw edge; ignore the selvages at the lower edge that may not line up perfectly with the horizontal ruler grid. A good rule of thumb to remember when rotary-cutting fabric is "the piece you want to keep should be under the ruler." That way, if you accidentally swerve away from the ruler when cutting, the piece under the ruler will be "safe."

3. Placing your rotary cutter along the ruler's right-hand edge and holding the ruler firmly with your left hand, run the blade along the ruler, as in Step 3 of Squaring Up the Fabric Edge, *left,* to cut the strip. Remove the ruler.

4. Sliding the excess fabric out of the way, carefully turn the mat so the 2" strip is horizontal in relation to you. Refer to Squaring Up the Fabric Edge to trim off the selvage edges and square up the strip's short edges.

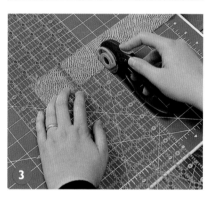

5. Align the ruler's 2" grid mark with a squared-up short edge of the strip (the 2" square you want to keep should be under the ruler). Hold the ruler with your left hand and run the rotary cutter along the right-hand ruler edge to cut a 2" square. To cut multiple 2" squares from one strip, slide the ruler over 2" from the previous cutting line and cut again (see **Photo 3**). From a 44/45"-wide strip, you'll likely be able to cut twenty-one 2" squares. Since in this example you need a total of 40, cut a second 2"-wide strip and subcut it into 2" squares.

CUTTING TRIANGLES

Right triangles also can be quickly and accurately cut with a rotary cutter. There are two common ways to cut triangles. An example of each method follows.

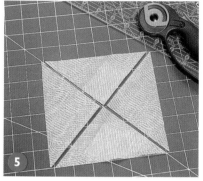

To cut two triangles from one square, the instructions may read:

From green print, cut:
- 20—3" squares, cutting each in half diagonally for 40 triangles total

1. Referring to Cutting and Subcutting Strips, *opposite*, cut a 3"-wide fabric strip and subcut the strip into 3" squares.

2. Line up the ruler's edge with opposite corners of a square to cut it in half diagonally (see **Photo 4**). Cut along the ruler's edge. *Note:* The triangles' resultant long edges are on the bias. Avoid stretching or overhandling these edges when piecing so that seams don't become wavy and distorted.

To cut four triangles from one square, the instructions may read:

From green print, cut:
- 20—6" squares, cutting each diagonally twice in an X for 80 triangles total

3. Referring to Cutting and Subcutting Strips, *opposite*, cut a 6"-wide fabric strip and subcut it into 6" squares.

4. Line up the ruler's edge with opposite corners of a square to cut it in half diagonally. Cut along the ruler's edge; do not separate the two triangles created. Line up the ruler's edge with the remaining corners and cut along the ruler's edge to make a total of four triangles (see **Photo 5**). *Note:* The triangles' resultant short edges are on the bias. Avoid stretching or overhandling these edges when piecing so that seams don't become wavy and distorted.

CUTTING WITH TEMPLATES

A successful quilt requires precise cutting of pieces.

About Scissors

Sharp scissor blades are vital to accurate cutting, but keeping them sharp is difficult because each use dulls the edges slightly. Cutting paper and plastic speeds the dulling process, so invest in a second pair for those materials and reserve your best scissors for fabric.

Make the Templates

For some quilts, you'll need to cut out the same shape multiple times. For accurate piecing later, the individual pieces should be identical to one another.

A template is a pattern made from extra-sturdy material so you can trace around it many times without wearing away the edges. You can make your own templates by duplicating printed patterns (like those on the Pattern Sheets) on plastic.

To make permanent templates, we recommend using easy-to-cut template plastic. This material lasts indefinitely, and its transparency allows you to trace the pattern directly onto its surface.

To make a template, lay the plastic over a printed pattern. Trace the pattern onto the plastic using a ruler and a permanent marker. This will ensure straight lines, accurate corners, and permanency. *Note:* If the pattern you are tracing is a half-pattern to begin with, you must first make a full-size pattern. To do so, fold a piece of tracing paper in half and crease; unfold. Lay the tracing paper over the half-pattern, aligning the crease with the fold line indicated on the pattern. Trace the half-pattern. Then rotate the tracing paper, aligning the half-pattern on the opposite side of the crease to trace the other half of the pattern. Use this full-size pattern to create your template.

For hand piecing and appliqué, make templates the exact size of the finished pieces, without seam allowances, by tracing the patterns' dashed lines. For machine piecing, make templates with the seam allowances included.

For easy reference, mark each template with its letter designation, grain line if noted, and block name. Verify the template's size by placing it over the printed pattern. Templates must be accurate or the error, however small, will compound many times as you assemble the quilt. To check the accuracy of your templates, make a test block before cutting the fabric pieces for an entire quilt.

continued

Trace the Templates

To mark on fabric, use a special quilt marker that makes a thin, accurate line. Do not use a ballpoint or ink pen that may bleed if washed. Test all marking tools on a fabric scrap before using them.

To trace pieces that will be used for hand piecing or appliqué, place templates facedown on the wrong side of the fabric; position the tracings at least ½" apart (see **Diagram 1**, template A). The lines drawn on the fabric are the sewing lines. Mark cutting lines, or estimate a seam allowance around each piece as you cut out the pieces. For hand piecing, add a ¼" seam allowance; for hand appliqué, add a ³⁄₁₆" seam allowance.

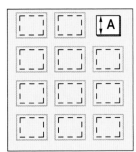

Diagram 1

Templates used to make pieces for machine piecing have seam allowances included so you can use common lines for efficient cutting. To trace, place templates facedown on the wrong side of the fabric;

position them without space in between (see **Diagram 2**, template B). Using sharp scissors or a rotary cutter and ruler, cut precisely on the drawn (cutting) lines.

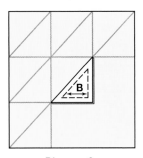

Diagram 2

Templates for Angled Pieces

When two patchwork pieces come together and form an angled opening, a third piece must be set into this angle. This happens frequently when using diamond shapes.

For a design that requires setting in, a pinhole or window template makes it easy to mark the fabric with each shape's exact sewing and cutting lines and the exact point of each corner on the sewing line. By matching the corners of adjacent pieces, you'll be able to sew them together easily and accurately.

To make a pinhole template, lay template plastic over a pattern piece. Trace both the cutting and sewing lines onto the plastic. Carefully cut out the template on the cutting line. Using a

sewing-machine needle or any large needle, make a hole in the template at each corner on the sewing line (matching points). The holes must be large enough for a pencil point or other fabric marker to poke through.

Trace Angled Pieces

To mark fabric using a pinhole template, lay it facedown on the wrong side of the fabric and trace. Using a pencil, mark dots on the fabric through the holes in the template to create matching points, then cut out the fabric piece on the drawn line.

To mark fabric using a window template, lay it facedown on the wrong side of the fabric (see **Diagram 3**). With a marking tool, mark the cutting line, sewing line, and each corner on the sewing line (matching points). Cut out the fabric piece on the cutting lines, making sure all pieces have sewing lines and matching points marked.

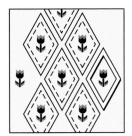

Diagram 3

PIECING

Patchwork piecing consists of sewing fabric pieces together in a specific pattern.

Hand Piecing

In hand piecing, seams are sewn only on the marked sewing lines; the seam allowances remain unstitched. Begin by matching the edges of two pieces with the fabrics' right sides together. Sewing lines should be marked on the wrong side of both pieces. Push a pin through both fabric layers

at each corner (see **Diagram 1**). Secure the pins perpendicular to the sewing line. Insert more pins between the corners.

Insert a needle through both fabrics at the seam-line corner. Make one or two backstitches atop the first stitch to secure the thread. Weave the needle in and out of the fabric along the seam line, taking four to six tiny stitches at

a time before you pull the thread taut (see **Diagram 2**). Remove the pins as you sew. Turn the work over occasionally to see that the stitching follows the marked sewing line on the other side.

Sew eight to 10 stitches per inch along the seam line. At the end of the seam, remove the last pin and make the ending stitch through the hole left by the corner pin.

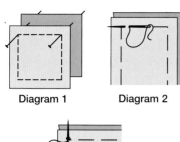

Diagram 1   Diagram 2

Diagram 3

Backstitch over the last stitch and end the seam with a loop knot (see **Diagram 3**).

To join rows of patchwork by hand, hold the sewn pieces with right sides together and seams matched. Insert pins at the corners of the matching pieces. Add additional pins as necessary, securing each pin perpendicular to the sewing line (see **Diagram 4**).

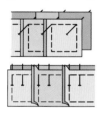

Diagram 4

Stitch the joining seam as before, but do not sew across the seam allowances that join the patches. At each seam allowance, make a backstitch or loop knot, then slide the needle through the seam allowance (see **Diagram 5**). Knot or backstitch again to give the intersection strength, then sew the remainder of the seam. Press each seam as it is completed.

Diagram 5

Machine Piecing

Machine piecing depends on sewing an exact ¼" seam allowance. Some machines have a presser foot that is the proper width, or a ¼" foot is available.

To check the width of a machine's presser foot, sew a sample seam with the raw fabric edges aligned with the right edge of the presser foot; measure the resultant seam allowance using graph paper with a ¼" grid.

Using two thread colors—one in the needle and one in the bobbin—can help you to better match your thread color to your fabrics. If your quilt has many fabrics, use a neutral color, such as gray or beige, for both the top and bobbin threads throughout the quilt.

Press for Success

In quilting, almost every seam needs to be pressed before the piece is sewn to another, so keep your iron and ironing board near your sewing area. It's important to remember to press with an up and down motion. Moving the iron around on the fabric can distort seams, especially those sewn on the bias.

Project instructions in this book generally tell you in what direction to press each seam. When in doubt, press the seam allowance toward the darker fabric. When joining rows of blocks, alternate the direction the seam allowances are pressed to ensure flat corners.

Setting in Pieces

The key to sewing angled pieces together is aligning marked matching points carefully. Whether you're stitching by machine or hand, start and stop sewing precisely at the matching points (see dots in **Diagram 6**, top) and backstitch to secure the ends of the seams. This prepares the angle for the next piece to be set in.

Join two diamond pieces, sewing between matching points to make an angled unit (see **Diagram 6**).

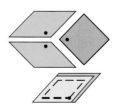

Diagram 6

Follow the specific instructions for either machine or hand piecing to complete the set-in seam.

MACHINE PIECING

With right sides together, pin one piece of the angled unit to one edge of the square (see **Diagram 7**). Match the seam's matching points by pushing a pin through both fabric layers to check the alignment. Machine-stitch the seam between the matching points. Backstitch to secure the ends of the seam; do not stitch into the ¼" seam allowance. Remove the unit from the sewing machine.

Bring the adjacent edge of the angled unit up and align it with the next edge of the square (see **Diagram 8**). Insert a pin in each corner to align matching points, then pin the remainder of the seam. Machine-stitch between matching points as before. Press the seam allowances of the set-in piece away from it.

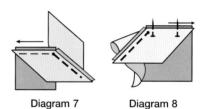

Diagram 7   Diagram 8

HAND PIECING

Pin one piece of the angled unit to one edge of the square with right sides together (see **Diagram 9**). Use pins to align matching points at the corners.

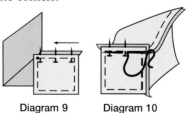

Diagram 9   Diagram 10

Hand-sew the seam from the open end of the angle into the corner. Remove pins as you sew between matching points. Backstitch at the corner to secure stitches. Do not sew into the ¼" seam allowance and do not cut your thread.

continued

Bring the adjacent edge of the square up and align it with the other edge of the angled unit. Insert a pin in each corner to align matching points, then pin the remainder of the seam (see **Diagram 10** on *page 155*). Continuing the thread from the previous seam, hand-sew the seam from the corner to the open end of the angle, removing pins as you sew. Press the seam allowances of the set-in piece away from it.

Mitered Border Corners

A border surrounds the piecework of many quilts. Mitered corners add to a border's framed effect.

To add a border with mitered corners, first pin a border strip to a quilt top edge, matching the center of the strip and the center of the quilt top edge. Allow excess border fabric to extend beyond the edges. Sew together, beginning and ending the seam ¼" from the

quilt top corners (see **Diagram 11**). Repeat with the remaining border strips. Press the seam allowances toward the border strips.

Overlap the border strips at each corner (see **Diagram 12**). Align the edge of a 90° right triangle with the raw edge of a top border strip so the long edge of the triangle intersects the seam in the corner. With a pencil, draw along the edge of the triangle from the border seam out to the raw edge. Place the bottom border strip on top and repeat the marking process.

With the right sides of adjacent border strips together, match the marked seam lines and pin (see **Diagram 13**).

Beginning with a backstitch at the inside corner, stitch exactly on the marked lines to the outside edges of the border strips. Check the right side of the corner to see that it lies flat. Then trim the excess fabric, leaving a ¼" seam allowance. Press the seam open. Mark and sew the remaining corners in the same manner.

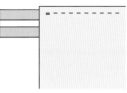

Diagram 11

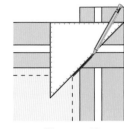

Diagram 12

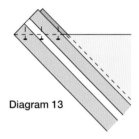

Diagram 13

APPLIQUÉ

With appliqué, you create a picture by stitching fabric shapes atop a fabric foundation.

Start Simple

We encourage beginners to select an appliqué design with straight lines and gentle curves. Learning to make sharp points and tiny stitches takes practice.

In the following instructions, we've used a stemmed flower motif as the appliqué example.

Baste the Seam Allowances

Begin by turning under the ³⁄₁₆" seam allowances on the appliqué pieces; press. Some quilters like to thread-baste the folded edges to ensure proper placement. Edges that will be covered by other pieces don't need to be turned under.

For sharp points on tips, first trim the seam allowance to within ⅛" of the stitching line

(see **Photo 1**, *opposite*), tapering the sides gradually to ³⁄₁₆". Fold under the seam allowance remaining on the tips. Then turn the seam allowances under on both sides of the tips. The side seam allowances will overlap slightly at the tips, forming sharp points.

Baste the folded edges in place (see **Photo 2**, *opposite*). The turned seam allowances may form little pleats on the back side that you also should baste in place. Remove the basting stitches after the shapes have been appliquéd to the foundation.

Make Bias Stems

For graceful curves, cut appliqué stems on the bias. The strips for stems can be prepared in various ways. For one method, fold and

press the strip in half, then fold the raw edges to meet at the center; press in half again as shown in **Photo 3**, *opposite*. Or, fold the bias strip in half lengthwise with the wrong side inside; press. Stitch ¼" from the raw edges to keep them aligned. Fold the strip in half again, hiding the raw edges behind the first folded edge; press.

Position and Stitch

Pin the prepared appliqué pieces in place on the foundation (see **Photo 4**, *opposite*) using the position markings or referring to the appliqué placement diagram. If your pattern suggests it, mark the position for each piece on the foundation before you begin. Overlap the flowers and stems as indicated.

Using thread in colors that match the fabrics, sew each stem and blossom onto the foundation with small slip stitches as shown in **Photo 5**. (For photographic purposes, thread color does not match fabric color.)

Catch only a few threads of the stem or flower fold with each stitch. Pull the stitches taut, but not so tight that they pucker the fabric. You can use the needle's point to manipulate the appliqué edges as needed. Take an extra slip stitch at the point of a petal to secure it to the foundation.

You can use hand-quilting needles for appliqué stitching, but some quilters prefer a longer milliner's or straw needle. The extra needle length aids in tucking fabric under before taking slip stitches.

If the foundation fabric shows through the appliqué fabrics, cut away the foundation fabric. Trimming the foundation fabric also reduces the bulk of multiple layers when quilting later. Carefully trim the underlying fabric to within ¼" of the appliqué stitches (see **Photo 6**) and avoid cutting the appliqué fabrics.

Fusible Appliqué

For quick-finish appliqué, use paper-backed lightweight fusible web. You can iron the shapes onto the foundation and add decorative stitching to the edges. This product consists of two layers, a fusible webbing lightly bonded to paper that peels off. The webbing adds a slight stiffness to appliqué pieces.

When purchasing this product, read the directions on the package to make sure you're buying the right kind for your project. Some are specifically engineered to bond fabrics with no sewing at all. If you try to stitch fabric after it has bonded with one of these products, you may have difficulty. Some paper-backed fusible products are made only for sewn edges; others work with or without stitching.

If you buy paper-backed fusible web from a bolt, be sure fusing instructions are included because the iron temperature and timing varies by brand. This information is usually on the paper backing.

With any of these products, the general procedure is to trace the patterns wrong side up onto the paper side of the fusible web. Then place the fusible-web pieces on the wrong side of the appliqué fabrics, paper side up, and use an iron to fuse the layers together. Cut out the fabric shapes, peel off the paper, turn the fabrics right side up, and fuse them to the foundation fabric.

You also can fuse the fusible web and fabric together before tracing. You'll still need to trace templates wrong side up on the paper backing.

If you've used a no-sew fusible web, your appliqué is done. If not, finish the edges with hand or machine stitching.

CUTTING BIAS STRIPS

Strips for curved appliqué pattern pieces, such as meandering vines, and for binding curved edges should be cut on the bias, which runs at a 45° angle to the selvage of a woven fabric and has the most give or stretch.

To cut bias strips, begin with a fabric square or rectangle. Use a large acrylic ruler to square up the left edge of the fabric. Then make a cut at a 45° angle to the left edge (see **Bias Strip Diagram**). Handle the diagonal edges carefully to avoid distorting the bias. To cut a strip, measure the desired width parallel to the 45° cut edge; cut. Continue cutting enough strips to total the length needed.

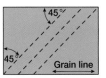

Bias Strip Diagram

COVERED CORDING

Finish pillows and quilts with easy, tailored cording.

Covered cording is made by sewing a fabric strip around a length of cording. The width of the strip varies according to the diameter of your cording. Refer to the specific project instructions for those measurements. Regardless, the method used to cover the cording is the same.

With the wrong side inside, fold under 1½" at one end of the strip. With the wrong side inside, fold the strip in half lengthwise to make the cording cover. Insert the cording next to the folded edge, placing a cording end 1" from the cording cover folded end. Using a cording foot or zipper foot, sew through the fabric layers right next to the cording (see **Diagram 1**).

When attaching the cording to your project, begin stitching 1½"

from the covered cording's folded end. As you stitch each corner, clip the seam allowance to within a few threads of the stitching line; gently ease the covered cording into place (see **Diagram 2**).

After going around the entire edge of the project, cut the end of the cording so that it will fit snugly into the folded opening at the beginning (see **Diagram 3**). The ends of the cording should abut inside the covering. Stitch the ends in place to secure (see **Diagram 4**).

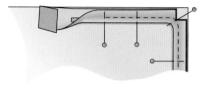

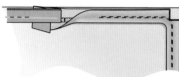

Diagram 2

Diagram 3

Diagram 1

Diagram 4

HANGING SLEEVES

When you want a favorite quilt to become wall art,

hang it with care to avoid sagging, tearing, and wavy edges.

Quilts make wonderful pieces of wall art. When treated as museum pieces and hung properly, they won't deteriorate. Let size be your guide when determining how to hang your quilt.

Hang smaller quilts, a 25" square or less, with purchased clips, sewn-on tabs, or pins applied to the corners. Larger quilts require a hanging sleeve attached to the back. It may take a few minutes more to sew on a sleeve, but the effort preserves your hours of work with less distortion and damage.

Make a Hanging Sleeve

1. Measure the quilt's top edge.

2. Cut a 6"- to 10"-wide strip of prewashed fabric 2" longer than the quilt's top edge. For example, if the top edge is 40", cut a 6×42" strip. A 6"-wide strip is sufficient for a dowel or drapery rod. If you're using something bigger in diameter, cut a wider fabric strip. If you're sending your quilt to be displayed at a quilt show, adjust your measurements

Diagram 1

Diagram 2

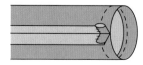

Diagram 3

Quilter's Schoolhouse

to accommodate the show's requirements.

3. Fold under 1½" on both ends of the fabric strip. Sew ¼" from the raw edges (see **Diagram 1**).

4. Fold the fabric strip in half lengthwise with the wrong side inside; pin. Stitch together the long edges with a ¼" seam allowance (see **Diagram 2**) to make the sleeve. Press seam allowance open and center the seam in the middle of the sleeve (see **Diagram 3**).

5. Center the sleeve on the quilt back about 1" below the binding with the seam facing the back (see **Diagram 4**). Slip-stitch the sleeve to the quilt along both long edges and the portions of the short edges that touch the back, stitching through the back and batting.

6. Slide a wooden dowel or slender piece of wood that is 1" longer than the finished sleeve into the sleeve and hang as desired.

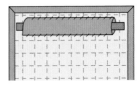

Diagram 4

COMPLETE THE QUILT

The final step in quiltmaking is to bind the edges.

Layering

Cut and piece the backing fabric to measure at least 3" bigger on all sides than the quilt top. Press all seam allowances open. With wrong sides together, layer the quilt top and backing fabric with the batting in between; baste. Quilt as desired.

Binding

The binding for most quilts is cut on the straight grain of the fabric. If your quilt has curved edges, cut the strips on the bias (see *page 157*). The cutting instructions for projects in this book specify the number of binding strips or a total length needed to finish the quilt. The instructions also specify enough width for a French-fold, or double-layer, binding because it's easier to apply and adds durability.

Join the strips with diagonal seams to make one continuous binding strip (see **Diagram 1**). Trim the excess fabric, leaving

¼" seam allowances. Press the seam allowances open. With the wrong sides together, fold under 1" at one binding strip end (see **Diagram 2**); press. Fold the strip in half lengthwise (see **Diagram 3**); press.

Beginning in the center of one side, place the binding strip against the right side of the quilt top, aligning the binding strip's raw edges with the quilt top's raw edge (see **Diagram 4**). Beginning 1½" from the folded edge, sew through all layers, stopping ¼" from the corner. Backstitch, then clip the threads. Remove the quilt from under the presser foot.

Fold the binding strip upward (see **Diagram 5**), creating a diagonal fold, and finger-press.

Holding the diagonal fold in place with your finger, bring the binding strip down in line with the next edge, making a horizontal fold that aligns with the first edge of the quilt (see **Diagram 6**).

Start sewing again at the top of the horizontal fold, stitching through all layers. Sew around the quilt, turning each corner in the same manner.

When you return to the starting point, lap binding strip inside the beginning fold (see **Diagram 7**). Finish sewing to the starting point (see **Diagram 8**). Trim the batting

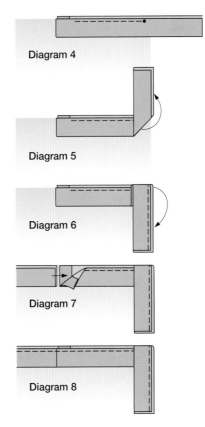

Diagram 4

Diagram 5

Diagram 6

Diagram 7

Diagram 8

and backing fabric even with the quilt top edges.

Turn the binding over the edge of the quilt to the back. Hand-stitch the binding to the backing fabric, making sure to cover any machine stitching.

To make mitered corners on the back, hand-stitch the binding up to a corner; fold a miter in the binding. Take a stitch or two in the fold to secure it. Then stitch the binding in place up to the next corner. Finish each corner in the same manner.

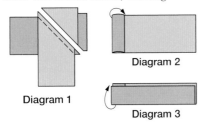

Diagram 1

Diagram 2

Diagram 3

CREDITS

Quilt Designers

Cindy Blackberg
Sweet Peas
A student of turn-of-the-century quilts, designer Cindy Blackberg combines designs and colors from antique quilts to create modern heirlooms.

Shirley Delph
Ali's Quilt
Professional designer and illustrator Shirley Delph enjoys pulling scraps from her large cache of fabric to create colorful and whimsical quilts for her loved ones.

Kim Diehl
Patchwork Primer
A self-taught quilter, Kim Diehl designs quilts that have homespun charm. She enhances traditional patterns with appliqué accents.

Becky Goldsmith and Linda Jenkins
Pink Pinwheels
Pattern designers Becky Goldsmith and Linda Jenkins of Piece O' Cake Designs collaborate on intricate appliqué quilts.

Julie Hendricksen
Thousand Pyramids and *Delectable Mountains*
Shop owner and designer Julie Hendricksen creates patterns based on her extensive collection of antique quilts.

Kris Kerrigan
Crowded Lake
Kris Kerrigan publishes her quilt designs under the Button Weeds label. Her projects in appliqué and pieced patchwork have a light-hearted, folk art appeal.

Mabeth Oxenreider
Trail Mix and *Heading North*
Teacher and award-winning quilter Mabeth Oxenreider uses multiple techniques—from foundation piecing to machine appliqué—to complete projects.

Cheryl Pedersen
Ohio Memories
Cheryl Pedersen, along with Nancy Bowen, designs quilt patterns using appliqué, pieced patchwork, and redwork techniques under the name Remembrances Two.

Lisa DeBee Schiller
Remember Me
Intricate layouts and appliqué are elements Lisa DeBee Schiller enjoys most in her pattern designs. Lisa designs patterns under the name Village Classics.

Tonee White
Signs of Spring
Quiltmaker Tonee White combines appliquéing and quilting in one step when she teaches her "appliquilt" technique.

Darlene Zimmerman
Boston Commons
Quilt designer and teacher Darlene Zimmerman is also the author of books and articles on quilting.

Laura Boehnke
Quilt Tester
With a keen color sense and an astute use of fabrics, Laura Boehnke gives each project in *American Patchwork & Quilting®* magazine an entirely different look from its original as she verifies its pattern.

Project Quilters and Finishers
Laura Boehnke: pages 42, 77, 97, 118
Kelly Edwards: pages 13, 14, 46, 54, 61, 62, 72, 80, 98, 106, 115, 145
Kate Hardy: pages 22, 24
Lisa Ippolito: pages 14, 145
Roseann Meehan Kermes: page 134
Mabeth Oxenreider: pages 34, 86
Mary Pepper: pages 88, 137, 149
Jan Ragaller: page 53
Nancy Sharr: pages 42, 77
Janelle Swenson: pages 70, 126, 129
Sue Urich: pages 42, 77, 97, 118
April West: pages 22, 24, 70, 88, 126, 129, 149

Materials Suppliers
Andover Fabrics
AvLyn Creations
Clothworks
Henry Glass & Co.
Hoffman Fabrics
Marcus Fabrics
Michael Miller Fabrics
Moda Fabrics
Red Rooster Fabrics
RJR Fabrics
Robert Kaufman Fabrics

Photographers
Marcia Cameron: pages 28, 29, 48, 74
Kim Cornelison: pages 19, 66
Jason Donnelly: pages 44, 96, 119
Hopkins Associates: pages 8, 11, 12
Scott Little: pages 55, 101, 103, 104, 116, 146
Greg Scheidemann: pages 13, 14, 16, 22, 24, 34, 42, 46, 53, 54, 61, 62, 70, 72, 77, 80, 83, 86, 88, 97, 106, 108, 115, 118, 126, 129, 134, 137, 145, 149
Perry Struse: pages 21, 27, 30, 32, 33, 38, 40, 41, 56, 59, 60, 92, 94, 111, 114, 122, 125, 130, 138, 142, 144, 150, 152, 153, 157
Steve Struse: pages 50, 51
Jay Wilde: pages 15, 25, 35, 73, 78, 79, 81, 85, 89, 128